Copyright © 2024 Briana Lawrence
All rights reserved

This book is memoir. It reflects the author's present recollections of experiences over time. Some names and characteristics have been changed, some events have been compressed, and some dialogue has been recreated.

No part of this book may be reproduced, or stored in a retrieval system, or transmitted in any form or by any means, electronic, mechanical, photocopying, recording, or otherwise, without express written permission of the publisher.

ISBN: 979-8-9907650-0-9

Cover design by: Amanda Cestaro
Printed in the United States of America

whenwewentsouth.com

WHEN WE WENT SOUTH

A memoir

BRIANA LAWRENCE

AMADA PRESS

TO LUCIA

WHEN WE WENT SOUTH

MILESTONES

April 11, 2014

The tiny sedan dashed past early morning revelers, my moans drowning out their drunken chatter. Between contractions, I scanned the streets I had grown used to, the sights that once felt so foreign but were now a new version of home: the grocery store where we'd spent our last pesos on roasted chicken and beer, the bus stop on the corner where I'd stood for hours over the past five years contemplating my loneliness, the cafe where we'd found out about my pregnancy. Victories and losses, moments strung together and flashing through my mind. I grasped the handle overhead with a shaking hand and clung to my laboring belly with the other.

Our entire existence here had been marked by change, milestone upon milestone stacked up to create a new life for the two of us. But we had always been separate in our experience, so very different in the ways Chile had changed us. Nearly our entire relationship took place here. And now, we had created a new life between us, one that would tie us to that place and each other forever.

In the weeks before her arrival, I wondered: Would she bring a new perspective? Could I finally feel at ease in my life in Chile, or would the finish line forever feel like it was being pushed further and further away the moment I attempted to cross it? My unspoken questions were always there, bubbling up into a nervousness he was tired of dealing with. And I was tired too.

Years later, when I'd look at her sometimes, a picture of Laguna Verde would paint itself in my mind—our little white house and the never-ending pines. The flames in the sky over Valparaiso on the day we brought her home.

COMMUTES

May, 2008

I scanned the crowded subway car, Paul Simon strumming in my ears. Everyone around me seemed perfectly content with their busy urban lives. They must be crazy, I thought. There had to be more to life than this back and forth, the commute to the office, the ten paid days of vacation, the pushing of paper, the paying of bills. Not that I was paying my bills, exactly. I still had my parents to thank for that. The music in my headphones and fuzzy daydreams were my only escape from reality, a reality that had basically lost its luster as quickly as it had started.

    I had followed along with the rest of the recent grads from my prestigious liberal arts college and gotten a nine to five job in New York City. But the job market was abysmal to say the least. Many of my friends from school had decided to get graduate degrees instead of entering the job market at the worst time in recent history. After graduation everyone around me seemed so sure of where they were headed while I, overwhelmed by endless options of places to move and careers to pursue, chose to accept the first job I was offered, which in my case was an entry level assistant role at a Public Relations company. There, my job consisted of traipsing around the city all day delivering lip gloss and nail polish to building attendants at the big magazine publishing houses. The women I worked with were ambitious, cutthroat even, and smarter than

I gave them credit for. They wanted to claw their way up the ladder in designer heels and I thought I would fit right in. But as much as I had been bred to focus on the way things looked, something in me had started to shift. I couldn't bring myself to care about the beauty products I was pitching, or imagine spending most of my waking hours talking about the latest nail polish color. I rode the subway all day watching the diverse humanity that filled the city, all the people rushing off to somewhere, and let my mind wander to other places.

As a kid I had always dreamed about living in New York—the idealized version of it I'd been sold, where I could afford a quirky apartment with the salary from a job in something fun and ambiguous, like "fashion" or "magazines." I imagined myself in stylish clothing with a cappuccino in my hand. But in all my childhood imagining, I hadn't exactly factored in a paycheck that would afford me said luxuries. And even though my parents were still thankfully subsidizing my apartment, they had tightened their purse strings around unnecessary purchases, like constant wardrobe updates and expensive drinks. So instead of glitzy evenings out, most nights I spent alone, eating a dinner of cheap crunchy peanut butter on toast in front of a movie in bed. Everything about my current existence made me feel like I was wearing someone else's life. And unlike everyone else I knew, I was beginning to realize I didn't want the thing I had signed up for.

While I stood, jammed face-to-face against the other commuters on my way uptown one night, the thought of moving to Argentina to teach English popped into my head. The idea hadn't sprung out of nowhere: I had been trying to return to a Spanish-speaking country since my study abroad days, but teaching in South America hadn't crossed my mind before that very moment. It was the first time in years that I felt thrust forward by something meaningful and the thought of it lit a fire that burned in my belly. I quit my job the next week and moved back to my parents' house in Pennsylvania. They were going through a messy, protracted divorce, but I had nowhere else to go. I wouldn't miss New York.

HOME
July, 2008

I was twenty-two, fresh off my first real fuckup, and back in my parents' house, the limbo-land between the past and the exciting future I had been assured lay before me. To fund my trip to Argentina, I had started waitressing at the Roadhouse, a cheesy franchise restaurant full of Texas-cowboy paraphernalia. My arrival back to Pennsylvania was too late in the summer to get any of the better service jobs, so I was stuck cowboy dancing, dreaming of November when I was planning to get the hell out of town. The only appealing part of the job, other than the easy paycheck, was that I never had to stay past 9 PM. Most nights I headed straight to the local dive bar to mingle with the other food industry folk. I enjoyed getting drunk and wanted companionship, so I faked my way through our mostly-superficial conversations, happy to drink my weight in Yuengling lager with the rest of the crew.

After my shift one night, I sat inside my car in the corner of the restaurant parking lot to get ready—I practically lived in my car that summer and it housed anything I could possibly need at a moment's notice: random bits of clothing, my favorite brand of light cigarettes, a two-piece swimsuit, a half-empty cup of Dunkin Donuts coffee. I don't remember ever eating much since caffeinated drinks and nicotine sustained me. I opened the mirror on the sun shield, hastily applied dark eyeliner around my wide blue eyes, smudged it just so. It was a look that got me attention, though mostly with the kind of men who had no intention of taking me out to dinner. I smacked my lips together with sticky pink gloss and shimmied my grease-stained jeans off in the driver's seat, replacing them with cutoffs.

The sun had just gone down but the humidity from the day still hung heavy in the air as I drove over to the dingy bar, which sat awkwardly between a residential neighborhood and a public golf course. I'd been frequenting this spot for years, long before I could use my real ID at the entrance. Standing in the door, I lit a cigarette in a way I had co-opted from movie stars, cupping the flame glamorously, and walked inside. As was customary, I scoped out the men surrounding the bar, until my gaze landed on him. I knew nearly everyone in this town, so a new face was obvious—he may as well have been bathed in a spotlight. His worn-out green baseball hat was turned down and blonde curls peeked out below the sides.

I chugged a quick beer, busying my hands by lighting another cigarette, and waited for my friends to arrive. As luck would have it, an old friend of mine started chatting to the stranger and casually waved me over. I could see the new guy wasn't interested in the conversation by the way he smoked, furiously sucking down Camel Lights. I approached. I couldn't see his face, but I noticed the black-inked graphic tattoo that decorated his tanned forearm. He looked tall. "I'm Bree," I threw out, my beer buzz shoring up my confidence. "Trey," he replied. He still seemed bored.

I could make out the shadow of his cheekbones from under his cap. Blonde stubble dotted his chin and I wondered how it would feel on my cheeks—scratchy, I imagined.

"Bree is looking to move to South America, bro, so I figure you two have something in common," my old friend said pointedly. I guess he had remembered a drunken conversation we'd had the week prior about my pending trip abroad.

I lit another cigarette and sat myself next to the mysterious man, doing my best impression of a self-assured woman who had better places to be than this seedy dive bar. Our matchmaker quietly peeled away, leaving us alone to assess each other.

I told him about the public relations job I had hated in Manhattan, my impending departure, and my plan to teach English to fund my travel in Argentina. I left out my parents' ongoing divorce, my dad's prescription drug problem, and my mom's withering away. I wanted to seem adventurous and fun. He didn't ask for my number when my girlfriends came to whisk me away so, afterwards, I didn't think twice about our encounter.

My dating history was anything but prolific, and my expectations were leisurely. I had been in and out of infatuation with the same boy for the better part of a decade, and once I realized my feelings for him were unrequited, had decided to stick to flings: the man I met at Pianos on the Lower East Side my last night in New York; an old friend from college who'd come to visit for a weekend; a chef who worked in a restaurant in town. These were experiences I could accumulate, like trophies, to prove how carefree I could be.

The next week I was sitting in front of the television at a girlfriend's house when an unknown number rang on my beat-up gray flip phone. Distracted by our conversation about the evening's plans, I let it go to voicemail. After deciding on a game plan for the night, our attention turned to my phone which was now dinging with a message. My girlfriends huddled around me as I pressed the speaker button on the playback prompt, and there he was—Trey, asking if we could meet again. Deciding not to play it cool, I called right back—but the line just rang.

"You've reached the voicemail box of Hilltop Farm." It was two voices, speaking slowly in unison. One of them sounded like the Marlboro man.

Did he live with his parents?

He eventually called back, and we planned to meet the next Friday night at the same bar. Despite the lackluster introduction, the mysterious man intrigued me.

The days passed slowly as I waited for the end of the week; it wasn't often I had plans worth looking forward to. Plus, the sexy stranger provided me with new material to fill my daydreams while I waited tables.

Finally, Friday arrived. Since it was a special occasion, I decided to wear my lucky green dress, which was short and flowy and had paid for itself in compliments. As I arrived at the bar, I lit a cigarette, threw my big brown leather bag across my shoulder like a shield, and walked in. My eyes quickly investigated the reaches of the dark room and U-shaped counter in search of him. I tried to seem casual, aloof even, though he was easy to spot, sitting quietly with a book in the corner, tall beer in hand, his hat turned down. Apparently looking mysterious was this guy's M.O. The signs of an adrenaline rush came over me, I felt my stomach drop and my heart rate quicken as I realized how handsome he actually was. Hoping to look like a woman who knew how to order a man's drink, I asked the surly bartender for a Black & Tan and sauntered toward him. I suddenly felt like a kid playing dress up.

"Hey there," he said. His aqua eyes, peeking up from his paperback, locked on mine. I was toast. I sat down next to him and circled the rim of my beer glass with my finger. Something about this meeting felt different than our first. We started our conversation where we had left off, but soon dispensed with small talk. I felt drawn to him, as if he had a gravitational pull I couldn't escape. I knew that I was leaving soon to move to Argentina, but I wondered if I might actually want to stick around a little longer now that I had met him.

He told me he had spent a semester in Chile during his master's degree program the year prior: "My degree's in foreign policy," he elaborated. "Though I don't see myself using it. Now I have over two hundred thousand dollars in student loan debt, and there's no way I'll ever pay that back."

I drained the remainder of my now-warm beer. My parents had paid for my college education in full and I had no concept of how much money two hundred thousand dollars actually was.

"I've been wanting to go to South America for years. I've finally run out of reasons not to," I said, not wanting to dwell on his obviously less-than-ideal financial situation. "Chile sounds beautiful—did you travel much?"

"Yeah—we traveled with the program, and then I traveled some on my own. There's so much to see there though, it's impossible to cover an entire country in just one visit."

"Did you see Argentina?" I asked, crossing my legs toward him.

"I did. They have the best food. It's like they're all Italians who speak Spanish, they're so animated, full of intensity and culture." He seemed so confident as he spoke. "You'll love it if you like that kind of thing."

What I wanted was for him to think I was the kind of person who liked that kind of thing.

"Were you in Buenos Aires? That's where I'm trying to go."

"Yup. That's about it, though—I didn't see much else of Argentina. Though I could tell you everything about Chile. Santiago at least. I spent a long month there. I was in a bad place but that's my fault. That was where I was. Not *where* I was, if you know what I mean," he said.

I wanted to know what he meant.

We spent that night in that darkened corner in a conversational ping-pong that felt like magic, a steady back and forth between the two of us. I listened with rapt attention as he described, in meticulous detail, the political history of Chile, the overthrow of Salvador Allende and the dictatorship of Pinochet. He complained that the master's in foreign policy had done him no good—he was now saddled with a mountain of student loan debt and no desire to become a lifelong academic or a cog in the machine. He had moved to California, then back home, then back again. He had jumped out of airplanes and lived alongside the indigenous people of Peru. He had gone to school, and dropped out, and gone back again. He had been to all the places I had, and then some. He was, by far, the most interesting man I had ever met. He also displayed a sadness I simultaneously loved and wanted to fix. When he told me that he wanted to write a book some day, I pictured myself as the muse of his narrative.

He was living at his parents' farm temporarily, he explained, until he sorted out what came next. His first marriage had ended only a year before and was short-lived. She was bossy and codependent and came from a large, tight-knit family, he said, but explained nothing more about what had transpired between them. And I didn't want to ask. I, too, was running from what I deemed a miserable, normal life spent at a desk job and his explanation seemed fair enough to me. I scrawled my name and number on the back of a hand wipe packet, even though I knew he already had it (he kept it in the ashtray of his red Toyota Tacoma until it was sold five years later). We kissed for the first time that night in the parking lot; the sky was lit up with stars as his strong hands pulled me in. I shook with nervous energy the entire drive home.

Later that week we spent a night on the back porch of his parents' farmhouse, our outdoor chairs turned toward each other, leaning in to talk softly so we wouldn't wake them. They were still running the farm after all.

"This song is about Janis Joplin," he mused, as we listened to "Chelsea Hotel." I had never heard of Leonard Cohen before.

I sipped my Belgian beer slowly. "I love it," I said. And I did.

Falling in love with him felt like a mix of sweet sadness and butterflies in my belly. Like the songs were true. It was happy torture, nighttime experiments in infatuation.

I was in love with all of it and all of him. Like the way he looked when he talked about wanting to leave the US to live a self-made life abroad: lit up. How he touched my cheek with the tips of his calloused fingers right before he kissed me. The fact that he seemed to know something about all the interesting things in the big, wide world. He was eight years older than me, which meant he was over thirty, and a real man in my estimation. After we had slept together, he read me quotes in bed from dog-eared pages that he said reminded him of me.

"I was trying to describe you to someone. You don't look like any girl I've ever seen before," he read from *Revenge of the Lawn* by Richard Brautigan. I hung on every word—I'm sure he knew. His confidence made me feel safe, and learning the things he knew made me feel worldly. He was an education.

A week later on my twenty-third birthday, he picked me up at my parents' house made of salmon-colored brick, the one my brother and I grew up in. My parents had built it in 1997 when they still had money to spend. The house was up for sale then, in 2008, where it would sit for another year while the market plummeted, and folks tried to scurry out from under homes they could no longer afford.

I opened the garage door to find him in a cream-colored blazer, crisp white shirt and jeans, his curly blonde hair finally uncovered.

It was the first time I had been invited on a legitimate date by an adult male over the age of twenty-five.

"I washed up," he said, proudly displaying clean hands that were normally stained with remnants from tomato picking and dirt.

"I did, too," I said. After much deliberation, I had purchased a black dress from a boutique the next town over and had spent over an hour putting myself together. When he pulled me in for a quick kiss, standing in my parents' laundry room, I nearly died of happiness.

My mother invited him in for a beer in our sprawling kitchen; it was their first time meeting and I did my best to push the conversation along quickly. My parents didn't usually like my boyfriends.

"What do you do for a living?" my father prodded, while he sat, looking disinterested, from an adjacent chair in the next room, his right leg draped over the chair arm in a show of masculine dominance. My dad wasn't the type to say the thing he was thinking out loud, but you always knew. He would spin his thinly-veiled criticism into a witty remark, a quick blip of a joke he would later defend as funny. I never really noticed it until I got older, mostly because my mom never argued or addressed it. But the month before I left for college out of state, they told us my dad had had an affair, and after that, I started to see him differently and, lately, I had stopped caring about pissing him off.

Today, though, I was interested in keeping the peace, and I had no clue how Trey would react to my dad's sizing him up. While I nervously waited for a passive aggressive exchange to begin, I stared at the refrigerator.

"I finished my master's at Georgetown this past year and have been helping my parents on their farm since then. Before that I was at a doctoral program in Brooklyn," Trey replied, with the confidence of a man who'd been asked that question before.

"And where are you two going tonight?" My dad was clearly unimpressed with Trey's illustrious academic history.

"The Farmhouse, right down the street. It's the nicest farm to table restaurant close-by and I'd like to get to know the chef, hopefully start selling them some veggies and meat from the farm. Plus, the food is incredible," he answered.

"Have fun," my dad said and we were free to go.

Trey had made our reservation in the dimly lit basement room by the bar, and we filled ourselves to the brim with pork belly and sweet breads, fresh summer salad and rich Port wine. It was my introduction to good food—not just food that tasted good, but food grown well and with purpose. Sitting next to a man who farmed, who could eloquently critique the state of our food system, provided a beautiful, new context to a dinner out. At the end of the night the two of us hopped into his red truck, giddy with the possibility of one another. I drunkenly pawed at the radio and heard the beginning of Cat Stevens' "Peace Train" echoing over the busted speakers and cranked the volume up as loud as I could. I looked over at him and he turned toward me and we belted out the lyrics in unison. We sang along and laughed like two carefree teenagers while we whipped up the back roads to his parents' farm.

The next morning I crept back inside my parents' house to find my mother staring out the kitchen window. I had wanted to slip in and back out again to avoid an awkward conversation about spending the night with my date because even though I was technically an adult, I was temporarily back under their roof which meant I had to answer to them. At the very least, I had to entertain their criticism.

"He's handsome. You have fun?" she asked, sipping sugary coffee through a cocktail mixing straw.

"Yup, the food was delicious."

She scanned me as if she wanted to prod more, but didn't, and I immediately felt dirty and ashamed because it was obvious where the night had ended. I made an excuse to leave and ran upstairs to change my clothes and figure out where I could escape to next.

ESCAPE

August, 2008

For the rest of that summer, Trey and I were inseparable. By day I would waitress, earning as many tips as I possibly could, and by night I'd meet up with him. He got his own place close to the farm and I unofficially moved in before the ink dried on the lease. Our little blue house (or gray, as he called it) was old and hadn't seen a decent renovation in decades. It sat right next to the Vera Cruz Fire Company which was manned by an assortment of old Pennsylvania Dutch firemen and women who owned the house and they were kind enough to give him a good rate on the monthly rent in exchange for not complaining about the piercing fire alarms that woke us up at all hours of the night. Beige shag carpeting blanketed the downstairs and Trey's black lab Japhy, my new roommate, made us a happy threesome.

I spun The Arcade Fire and Band of Horses records on repeat on a little record player he bought me while I daydreamed about our future together. Books were arranged throughout every room in little piles, titles in Spanish and English he had amassed during his years spent on higher education. When I was alone in the house, I would page through them, looking for a glimpse of who he had been before me. He alluded to the life he had lived in his twenties, but I had to know more. I scrutinized over each note that was scrawled in the margins, each phone number written in the table of contents. Where had he been before me, and with whom? And was I good enough, smart enough, and beautiful enough to count myself among the women he had spent time with? My imagination ran away with me every time I discovered something new. It seemed like he had lived lifetimes in the eight years that separated us.

While we were in bed together one night I asked, "How many people have you been with?" Arguably one of the worst questions to ever ask a romantic partner.

"Hundreds," he replied, without blinking.

In an instant, I thought about all the women that came before me—all gorgeous, equally mysterious, probably academics. There was no way I could ever measure up.

Then, as if on cue, the dog clumsily knocked into the music speaker we had set up in the bedroom and Al Green's "Let's Get it On" began to play. I softened, laughed, and he was mine again. It felt as close to perfect as I knew.

"I love you," I whispered, just loud enough for him to hear me. The soft blue blanket was draped over the two of us.

"I love you too," he replied.

We had known each other for three months. But I saw in him a life full of adventure. We talked about all the places we could go to escape from the US. The job market at home was bleak and neither of us had any intention of being working stiffs anyway. He'd rather jump off a cliff than punch the clock.

"I want to build my own house and live off the land," he said one night.

We always had our best conversations on the porch, summer cicadas buzzing around us.

"I want to live in a Spanish-speaking country. My Spanish is pretty good actually," I responded.

He ventured inside and back out again, holding a guidebook to Mexico in his hand. "Costa Rica is supposed to be nice. I love Oaxaca. Or Chile. If we're together we can make anywhere work." He flipped open the book and cracked a beer. His words hung in the air—tiny promises that cemented me to him.

We survived on cigarettes and cheap thin crust pizza from the shop on the corner. He burned me CDs full of his favorite music.

We cuddled up on the worn-out 1970s couch and watched *The Royal Tenenbaums* over and over, in love with their colorful world and each other.

Trey and I were as devoted to our drinking habits as we were to one another. We would start on red wine early, drinking Cabernet Sauvignon out of coffee mugs in the greenhouses on the farm, then switching to beers halfway through the day. I'd chain-smoke cigarettes and watch him work while trying to appear useful. And he really got shit done, despite the drinking.

For the most part, we only displayed the best versions of ourselves. But he could be mercurial, and occasionally, his temper would flare when things didn't go his way—just like he told me his father's did. He'd throw a phone against the wall if it wasn't working, or slam down a computer so hard it would break. In early October, the local butcher came out to the farm to slaughter the pigs and the gunshot scared the dog so badly he ran away. Trey stomped and screamed, cursing loudly as I stood by and watched. It was the first time I remember his anger making me nervous, and embarassed. But his mood would improve just as quickly as it had turned sour and before I knew it he'd be passionately discussing his plans for the farm, enveloping me in his excitement.

I was young, in-love and all-in on our relationship, which meant I would do anything to protect it. Unfortunately, that left me in a predicament, seeing as I'd committed to leaving Pennsylvania at the end of the fall for my trip abroad. I could stay with Trey and forego my trip, or leave and miss out on him. I mulled over my options for weeks but even though this relationship seemed different than the others, I knew if I didn't prioritize travel, I might never have the opportunity again. So I decided to leave and started spreading the news among my friends. My college roommate, Callie, asked if she could come along for the journey too, so we both bought tickets to Argentina departing in October. I had managed to save up just enough money to cover the ticket in addition to about two month's rent while the rest of the trip would have to be paid for on credit. I didn't know how to break the news to him that I had actually planned my departure, so I waited, trying to figure out the perfect time.

On a crisp Sunday, he went to the farmer's market alone. The farm season was finally slowing down and he said he could manage by himself. He returned hours later, bounding up the stairs of our little gray house with an alpaca scarf he had bought us slung over his shoulders. He was still tan from the Indian summer and I was still so crazy about him I could barely see straight, let alone communicate something that I knew would disappoint him. But I couldn't wait any longer. I said that I still intended to leave, which he knew, but that I had finally booked my flight for Buenos Aires. As a sort of compromise, my plan for a one way ticket to adventure and self-discovery had been whittled down to a four month stint with a return date in February. I was terrified that in my absence he would move on and forget about me.

"Do what you gotta do," he said, and added: "I'm excited for you." And though he didn't stop loving me, there was a shift after that, maybe only perceptible by me. It felt like I had joined the ranks of all the people who had come before me that had disappointed him.

My departure couldn't have come at a better time. At home, my dad continued to contest the divorce with my mom. To make matters worse, he had lost his job where he had worked for nearly thirty years. Mom said it was because his prescription drug use had gotten too obvious and he simply wasn't working. Dad said he was going to sue them for wrongful termination. Mom hid herself within the confines and nooks of our big house, silently contemplating something I couldn't understand at the time. I both wished she would let me in and wanted her to just pretend like everything was fine. Dad spent most of his time in bed, or clicking away on a computer keyboard alone in his darkened office. The only time they spent together was on the cigarette breaks they shared in our three-car garage. I remember my mom's shoulders squared off and small, her arms folded over herself in protection, as if her days consisted of walking over a minefield trying not to set anything off, so thin she looked like she would break. His eyes were shifty and wandering, and his unpredictability made all of us nervous. I had never seen my dad lose his temper with her, but I knew enough about drugs to know that they changed you.

He was turning into someone I didn't know. I promised myself I wouldn't ever find myself in the same position, a woman trapped in her own home, getting through the days the only way she knew how. I couldn't imagine spending the holidays watching them unravel more than they already had and I was glad I wouldn't have to.

When the time had come to leave, I packed all of my bright summer things in my suitcase, loaded it in the back of Trey's red truck, and headed to the airport, a mix of guilt and excitement co-mingling in my belly while the winter grey sky hung overhead. I looked for a way to make easy conversation as he navigated the eastbound highway through the city, but nothing came to mind, so we sat in silence. I watched the loud billboards come and go through my passenger side window, wondering what this trip had in store for me.

We kissed goodbye in the departures section of JFK as hot tears streamed down my face and we promised to talk as much as we could. But I couldn't deny that I felt a sense of relief at leaving, at being able to shape shift again into something else. A single traveler, a young person without the burden of ties to family or relationships. Not a girlfriend, not a daughter. It meant I could move through the world however I wanted, whatever that meant. Callie would meet me in Miami and we'd be in Buenos Aires by morning.

WANDERING

October, 2008

We touched down in Buenos Aires on a spring day, leaving late fall behind, and quickly flagged down a taxi driver. *Hola*, I said, excited to practice my Spanish. I opened my tan leather journal to the page where I had written down the address of our hostel. We were staying in Palermo Soho, an area downtown which had been described online as a "hip neighborhood" and I was anxious to ditch our suitcases and start exploring. The two of us took in the sights from the roll-down windows of the taxi as we got moving—first, the dull highway and billboards advertising Argentine beers and home improvement stores, then as our driver took us further into the outskirts of the city, little homes and workshops with cracked facades dotted the sides of the street, all lined up in muted colors. Once we had neared our destination, about forty minutes into the drive, fashion boutiques began to appear, followed by quirky restaurants on cobblestone streets and small parks full of families with wide-eyed, obvious tourists.

We were exhausted, and starving too—we hadn't eaten since we had devoured a plate of overpriced nachos in the Miami airport the night prior. Faces pressed against the dirty cab window, we squealed at each other as our excitement grew with each passing block. We were already planning to go out and explore that night, our guidebooks were practically bursting with dog-eared pages of the city's best clubs and bars. The driver pulled up to a busy pedestrian intersection, we paid him a hefty tip, which we later learned was not customary, and waltzed into the hostel dragging our luggage behind us.

The building looked to be at least a hundred years old, with dark wooden floors and arched windows that stretched from floor to ceiling. We checked into our dorm room which housed at least six bunk beds overflowing with signs of life: books and dirty clothing, cigarette packets, journals, shampoo bottles. People popped in and out of the room as we placed our passports and other valuables into hiding places and shoved everything else under one of our beds.

That night we ventured out into the early summer evening and the hot night air on my skin felt like magic in late October. We spent the evening at a sparkling rooftop bar with a friend from college who we hadn't seen in years—Dan—who coincidentally was in Buenos Aires on a rotary scholarship. Over surprisingly inexpensive cocktails he gave us the lowdown on the best bars, neighborhoods, and restaurants in town, since he had been living in the city for the previous five months or so. He advised us that the grass fed steak at the touristy restaurant Don Julio would be the best of our life and to always eat the *chimichurri*, a sauce made of garlic, red wine vinegar, and parsley that was as much a staple food as the meat itself. "People go out here a lot," he said. "You could go out every night of the week, if you wanted to. And if you do, the fruit smoothies, they're called *licuados,* they'll cure your hangover, guaranteed." He cautioned us that Argentines, despite the heavy Italian influence, made some of the worst pizza he had ever tasted. "They put entire olives on it!" he exclaimed, "and the cheese is abysmal. I can't say it's even mozzarella. Just steer clear of it." We thanked him for the advice and returned to our hostel in the early hours of the morning (as was the norm for South American evenings out), thrilled by the newness of the place and all of the foreign experiences that lay before us.

Our hostel was inhabited by young people from all over the world: Brazil and Australia, the US and Italy. There were a number of open air common areas that were perfect for co-mingling with the other guests, which was probably the point, so in the morning, we made our way to the rooftop in the hopes of finding new friends. We didn't need to speak the same language to communicate—hand gestures, context, and friendliness, I quickly learned, would facilitate nearly every interaction. The first people we met were Andrew, an Argentine who was traveling with an American named Matt, and Jose, a Mexican who had spent his formative years in California. The three of them were as unencumbered as we were; they had met in their travels and were spending an indeterminate amount of time roaming around South America. We five became fast friends.

Eventually Callie and I moved out of the hostel and into the apartment of a friend for a couple of weeks until we found a more permanent place of our own. The woman who lived there was out of town and the second floor walk-up was the perfect location from which to explore. During the day we would meet up with the boys, maps in hand, to roam the city. It didn't take long to fall in love with Buenos Aires. It felt like a spread-out New York, a big city with breathing room. Each neighborhood had a personality: Upscale Recoleta with its famous cemetery; San Telmo with its antiques and street dancers and bohemian bookstores; Palermo Soho, full of irreverent boutiques and cafes; La Boca, a tourist trap for sure, but also beautifully set along the river and steeped in tango and history. I was also robbed there, my favorite gold necklace ripped from my neck in front of a busy subway station.

I learned how to make a proper *mate*, swirling in sticky-sweet Argentine orange juice to cut down on the bitterness of the black tea. Everyone there drank it hot, no matter the temperature outside. At night we plowed through bottles of Fernet Branca with Coca-Cola, and smoked Lucky Strikes as we paraded ourselves through the town's nightclubs and bars with whoever wanted to join in on the fun. We stayed out until morning and walked home as the sun was rising while we talked about the things that matter to twenty-three year olds, like love and work and sex. We were trying on all sorts of different lives, of which this was one, to see what fit. This foreign place was the perfect backdrop for the latest iteration of ourselves.

I was anxious to see more of Argentina, so a few weeks into our trip, the five of us booked an overnight bus, eighteen hours each way, to Iguazu Falls in the north. This series of waterfalls is one of the Seven Wonders of the World and creates the border between the Argentine province of Misiones and the Brazilian state of Paraná.

We boarded the double-decker bus, backpacks sagging under the weight of their contents—wine bottles, snacks and guidebooks, swimsuits hastily shoved into any space that remained. There was no need for more than a few articles of clothing.

Callie and I bounded up the awkward stairs to the second level and occupied two seats in the very front. The boys followed, taking their places in a raucous conversation punctuated by the throwing of various objects across the aisle. After what felt like a never-ending ride, "Holy shit guys, we're finally here," I announced, noticing the bus crawling off the highway exit and into town. We slid off one by one in a sleepy, sweaty huff into the busy bus terminal. It was early summer in the southern hemisphere and the north of the country had already turned impossibly hot.

"Now where the hell is the hostel?" someone asked.

"I think it's this way," another said, pointing toward a skinny road.

We found the hostel easily after a few twists and turns. To our surprise, it looked like we were some of the only visitors there. Maybe we were early for tourist season, we surmised, though the pool was full of water and brightly colored floats. The remainder of the morning's breakfast offerings: a pink-hued juice, instant coffee, and one lonely *medialuna* sat on a turquoise tray on a counter.

Out of nowhere, a man appeared from behind the tiki bar.

"Going out tonight?" he asked in a heavy accent.

He was handsome (as most Argentine men were in my opinion), with tan skin and thick dark hair that reached his shoulders.

"*A donde?*" I said, in my best Spanish.

He rattled off a reply I struggled to understand.

"What are y'all saying!" Callie exclaimed. "Y'all" was the last vestige of Callie's southern accent that remained from her childhood in Virginia. I thought it was cute.

Jose, far more fluent in Spanish than the rest of us, quickly took over the conversation and we trusted him to act as social coordinator for the evening. "We're all heading to a club later, there's one right in town," Jose said after discussion with the Argentine. "He said this place gets rowdy," he added.

As night came, the hostel's inhabitants came out of hiding, having apparently been sleeping off their hangovers by day in the large shared *dormitorios*. Reggaeton was turned all the way up on the speakers outside. The heat fell off the day and a chill crept into the desert air. Someone bought red wine in boxes and cheap *Quilmes*, the national beer, and started to pass drinks around community-style. Two long-haired hippies swung idly on a hammock while the smell of weed filled the night air.

"*Pa arriba pa abajo pa centro pa dentro!*" "Up, down, to the center, drink!" everyone screamed, delighted in our mastery of a new way to say "Cheers!"

Jose and I broke off from the larger group as we later stumbled our way to the *boliche*.

"Why are you dating someone back at home while you're here?" He asked.

"We met right before I was supposed to leave, and it got serious quickly."

At home, I had been reluctant to talk about the relationship with my friends for fear of being judged for how quickly we had jumped into being a couple. I had a tendency to dive into things, relationships included. You could say I didn't think much about the long term. I was still committed to Trey and steadfast in the belief that there was something special between us but right now, the new faces and places around me were intriguing.

"But are you happy with him?" He threw his arm around my shoulder.

"Yes, he's great," and I laughed to cover up the awkward turn in the conversation. Jose and I were friends, sure, but at the same time, I didn't want him to lose any romantic interest he had in me—attention was always welcome.

The night ended with me carefully dodging an aggressive come-on from the man from behind the tiki bar who turned out to be the manager of our hostel, and us dragging ourselves home as the sun came up. I had somehow managed to lose a flip flop, I realized, as I threw myself into the twin bed next to Callie.

Thankfully our twenty-three-year-old bodies ably handled our hangovers the next morning and we set off for the famous Iguazu falls, chugging Gatorade along the way. We walked a ways into the park, which looked unassuming enough at the start, but as we ventured further into the jungle, the immensity of the park silenced us. There were a number of routes leading to various points in the falls, from the cascading water of the Iguazu River down to the Parana River below. We chose the upper circuit first, a set of trails that showcase the beauty of the falls from all sides.

Lush greenery sprang out of every inch along the meandering path. Butterflies in the hundreds, in a myriad of shapes and colors, scattered across surfaces and fluttered all around us. They boldly landed on our outstretched arms, then flew off to be replaced by others. The trails turned into outlooks that hung high above the water below and we ran from one to another, drenched and giggling like little kids as we caught butterflies in our hands. Rainbows appeared in the mist coming off the falling water and small brown birds flew in and out of the falls. Between the blue sky and the rushing white water, everywhere we turned was deserving of a photo, but no image on my digital camera could capture the feeling of being there.

When we had finished the upper route, we made our way to the passenger train that would take us to the *Garganta del Diablo*, the largest and most impressive waterfall in the park.

The sounds of the rainforest surrounded us when we arrived but as we walked down wooden-planked trails that led toward the Garganta, the sound of rushing water overtook our senses. The five of us shuffled along and eventually arrived at the suspended walkway that hung directly in front of the massive, horseshoe-shaped falls. Water fell in sheets off the cliff with an otherworldly force unlike anything I had seen before. I had read that the falls were created two hundred million years before by a volcanic eruption, which was incomprehensible to me. What an incredible thing to be witness to, something so ancient and alive. And in the presence of such awesome beauty, my little life came into sharp focus. I felt small but free. I let my friends continue ahead to take pictures while I sat down on a bench alone, remembering my dialogue with Jose from the day before. Thoughts piled into my head, unwanted, contradicting. I loved Trey and was thankful to be with him. I was too young to be held down. I wanted stability. I needed freedom. I didn't know which voice to trust. *What was true?*

"Bree, come on!" Callie shouted in my direction. "We're taking a boat ride through the falls."

So I let the voices dissipate into the background and ran off after her.

After an eventful few days in Iguazu, we returned to Buenos Aires, once again grateful that our perpetual hangovers were the sort you could easily sleep off during a full-day bus ride.

About a month into our trip, Callie and I rented an expensive one-bedroom apartment in Alto Palermo, a quiet area with shops and tree-lined streets that smelled of fresh baguettes every morning. Even though we'd still be traveling plenty, we needed a home base in Buenos Aires for the remainder of our three month stay. Through Dan, we found a Realtor who most likely ripped us off, since we were tourists with little knowledge of the market and only moderate Spanish fluency. We paid the security deposit and two months' rent in one shot, which effectively drained my entire savings. Regardless of the fact that it wasn't the most sound financial decision, we loved our little apartment. I'd sit on the balcony and flip through my Lonely Planet guide while I lazily smoked, ashes dropping all over the terracotta-colored floor because I couldn't be bothered to buy an ashtray. When we weren't traveling, we were planning—we'd make sure we went to Patagonia, Mendoza, maybe even Uruguay if time didn't run out. And I desperately wanted to experience Chile, Argentina's skinny neighbor to the west.

There was an internet cafe three doors down that I visited nearly every day, to buy cigarettes or use the internet or both. I'd anxiously click open the browser to Gmail and hope to see an email from Trey. Sometimes there would be three in a row—he'd been drinking, and alone, and there wasn't enough farm work to keep him busy during the dead of winter. Then, an email to tell me he loved me and that he had never felt so understood by anyone as he had been by me. He had paid my credit card off, he was putting down new flooring in the bathrooms. He was building a life for us to inhabit as soon as I got back. Then, he'd remember that he felt like people were always leaving him.

"I'm just trying to understand why you still left," he'd write.

"I'm an idiot, I'm sorry," I'd respond, hoping to impart as much meaning as I could into a typed sentence across space.

"I love you so much, please forgive me. I'll never leave you again."

Our foundation was crumbling and I wanted to hang on tight. When I felt like splurging on a calling card, I called him.

"I hate this," I offered every time we spoke.

"It's not fair for me to ruin your time there, I'm sorry. This just sucks, I hate it here, it's cold and I might be worth running away from," he said. The connection was full of static and I could barely hear him.

"Then come here—you can come visit for a while and take a break. I love you. Please," I begged.

"Maybe, yeah. Now go have fun with Callie. I love you." Click. He booked a ticket to arrive right before Thanksgiving.

I couldn't bear any more emails or phone calls. In an attempt to embody how much I missed him and exert some control over a situation that felt shaky, I had all but given up eating. My relationship with food had been fraught since I was a teenager, and though I had grown out of the worst of it, I was still hyper-aware of my eating habits. An overindulgence, an unflattering photo, or a tight pair of jeans had the ability to throw me into a spiral of self-loathing. It felt comforting to fall back on an old habit.

By late November, summer had come to Buenos Aires and the streets were bustling with tourists and residents alike, the energy of the season palpable, but I woke up nervous on the day of his arrival. I put on a pair of skin-hugging white pants and a white top, grabbed a peach from the tiny fridge in the kitchen, and plopped myself down outside the gate to our apartment. I waited for him to arrive with the energy of a kid on Christmas morning. I plucked at the skin of the peach and lit myself a cigarette, the sticky juice coated my fingers and stained the lap of my pants.

Car after car rattled down our street, all the little imported

Peugeots and Citroens (because narrow streets call for tiny vehicles). With each car that slowed, my breath caught in my throat. It had only been a little over a month since I had last seen him, but it felt like much longer. A yellow cab turned the corner of Calle Billinghurst and slowly came to a stop in front of me. Wisps of his blonde curls were visible through the driver's side window. I jumped to my feet, dusted off my pants, and walked slowly toward him. He seemed like a mirage—the man in the computer, the one I'd fallen in love with that summer, was in Argentina. He smiled at seeing me, turned and threw the cab driver the pesos he owed, and in perfect Spanish, bid the driver goodbye.

"You're here!" I screamed and jumped into his arms.

"I am! Finally," he sighed.

I clutched the little red vintage suitcase he had brought, filled with goodies from the States. I had explicitly asked for both English muffins and sriracha hot sauce.

I bounced up the stairs to the second floor, forgoing the elevator that was perpetually stuck, Trey trailing right behind me.

"Hellooooo," I bellowed inside our sunny apartment and saw the breeze fluttering the floor-length drapes. I was anxious about introducing Callie to Trey.

Callie appeared from the galley kitchen, "Well, hi!" she said, stretching a hand to shake, always the polite southerner.

"How's it going? Nice to meet you," he said.

"There's an outdoor concert downtown tonight, Jose and the guys want to go with us."

"Yes! Let's go—you into that?" I asked him.

"I'm down," he answered.

"I'll go out and grab a bottle or two of wine, you guys can have some alone time," Callie said and winked.

We thought she'd never leave.

I tugged on his pants and dragged him into the bathroom, nearly ripping his shirt as I pried it off his head. He undressed me slowly, like he was enjoying every inch he had been missing, and started the shower. Hot water poured over the two of us in the pink-tiled bathroom as we fit ourselves back together.

"I never want to be without you again," he whispered, his

mouth on my neck. Shampoo bubbles slid down my shoulders.

"I never want to be without you, either." I heard the apartment door tick open and we scurried into the only bedroom in tiny towels then got dressed lazily, savoring each other's company at last. Once we admitted we couldn't stay in the bedroom all afternoon we ran out for a pack of cigarettes and another bottle of wine.

As we walked, he draped his arm over my shoulder. We had never been on vacation together, let alone in a foreign city, and it made Buenos Aires feel like an entirely new place with him by my side. I wondered if people could tell how happy we were when we passed them on the street. Once my apartment came into view he stopped walking purposefully and let go of my arm.

"What's going on, are you okay?" I asked.

"Yes, no, I just—I can't live without you. I want to ask you something," he said cryptically. "Can I take you shopping?"

"What are you talking about?"

"You know I want to be with you forever, Briana. Let's go buy a ring," he said, the words finally materializing.

"Oh my god—YES!" There was only one acceptable answer.

He wrapped his arms around me as we stumbled into the crisp white foyer of the apartment building and made our way toward the elevator. He threw open the metal gate, pressed #2, and held the emergency STOP button as soon as we were in between floors so we could celebrate, just the two of us, quickly enough not to get caught. I smoothed down my green dress to look presentable again just as I heard the neighbor's footsteps echoing from down the hall.

I swung open the apartment door, shouting, "We're engaged!" to our new friends who had all congregated in our living room to pre-game.

"Cheers, Rockstar!" Jose was the first one to speak, then Callie shouted, "Oh my god Bree!" Shock was plain on her face.

Just like that, we settled into our new normal. The twosome Callie and I had forged was now forced into a triangle. I hoped that she and Trey would get along.

THREE'S A CROWD

November, 2008

"Beep, beep!" Dan poked his head out of the driver's side window from across the street. "Over here!" he said, flagging us down from his grey car. The three of us, Callie, me, and Trey, crossed the intersection in front of the train station and squeezed into the tiny sedan Dan had rented for the weekend. I wiped the sweat that had accumulated on my brow and thanked him for the ride. Dan and his group of expat friends had invited us to a two-day Thanksgiving getaway in the town of Tigre, which was situated thirty minutes north of Buenos Aires along a stretch of water called the Parana Delta, an easy day trip from the city. We had boarded the slow-moving Tren de la Costa, and arrived an hour later ready to party. Through the train window I watched the landscape change from city to country and wondered what my family was doing back home. I missed them, but if I called I would have to explain my recent engagement, and I wasn't ready to do that yet.

All of the other guests were busy enjoying themselves when we arrived, spread out between a few rented cabins, the outdoor pool, and an empty pavilion that sat in the middle of a large grassy courtyard. After introductions, we spent the day drinking wine out of plastic cups in the swimming pool and prepping for dinner. Everyone was in various stages of inebriation and after a while Trey seemed to be enjoying himself, paddling around the perimeter of the pool with a bottle or a glass in hand, jumping from one conversation to the next. I'd catch a snippet about his work, or him discussing his degrees, and sneak in a kiss between breaks in the dialogue. I was proud to be with him. I thought he could hold his own with anyone.

When the sun went down we all found seats along a large table flanked by uncomfortable wooden benches and started passing around bowls overflowing with comfort food. It felt strange eating turkey and stuffing while wearing a wet bathing suit. To my left sat Trey, whose demeanor had suddenly taken a turn from gregarious to sullen, though I wasn't sure why. Out of the ambient chatter I heard a voice suggest we take turns sharing what we were thankful for and Dan stood up.

"Cheers to Trey and Bree—they just got engaged!" He nearly spilled his wine in his enthusiasm for the dramatic toast. I looked to Trey with my raised glass, but his eyes were glazed over and his lips were pursed into a pensive and angry look—I could feel everyone staring, so I touched his back to get his attention.

"Thanks guys—all good!" he said as he raised his glass to meet mine and the attention shifted from us. At least my turn had been skipped.

"Let's go to bed," I offered after we had cleaned our plates. We had both had too much to drink by then, so we made our way to a spot on the floor of a cabin and I covered us up with a random blanket I found draped over a couch.

"I don't deserve you, I'm going to fuck this up," he mumbled under his breath.

"What are you even talking about? That's not true."

"You left me, and you're having fun here, and I just mess everything up. I shouldn't have come, I shouldn't—"

He fell asleep mid-sentence and started snoring.

I could hear laughter outside, drunken voices telling stories. They sounded like they were having fun. It took me hours to fall asleep that night. I kept thinking about the people outside, and the things I was choosing or losing in order to be with him.

We kept ourselves busy for the next two weeks, though Trey's departure date loomed silently, reminding us that our time together had an expiration date. In Bariloche, Callie, Trey and I kayaked on a glacial lake and lingered in a *cerveceria*, sipping German-style beer from frosty mugs. We bought Cuban cigars and stared through the wide windows of our fancy hotel room at the white-capped mountains of the southern Andes. I had never been to Germany but was sure it looked something like that little town in Patagonia. Then we bused down to Puerto Madryn, the southernmost stop on our trip, for a whale watching tour that Callie had booked for us all. She was beside herself with excitement but Trey had other thoughts about the excursion, as evidenced by the scowl he wore while we boarded the little fishing boat headed out onto the Atlantic.

"What's wrong with him?" she asked me.

"Oh, I don't know, I'm sure he's fine, maybe he's just tired," I answered.

"You okay?" I asked him quietly, to confirm what I already knew.

"Yeah, this is just not what I want to be doing. It's not really my thing," he said. He was wearing a green leather jacket we had bought on credit at a boutique in Buenos Aires and bright white Chuck Taylors. He looked the part of someone who gave zero shits about whale watching. As we bounced on waves, searching for whales among excited tourists, I sat awkwardly beside my fiance and best friend, realizing I'd be playing interference between the two of them for the rest of the trip. Because I had brought the three of us together, I took it upon myself to make sure everyone was happy.

From Patagonia we headed north to Mendoza, the most famous wine region in the country, known for its robust red Malbec varietal. Once there, we booked a bike and wine "tour" where the "tour operator," an old man in a tiny roadside house, handed us rickety old bikes and a paper map, then waved us off. We drunkenly cruised down busy highways and side streets, searching out the vineyards on the brochure and sneaking into guided tour groups for the free wine tastings. The following day we rode horses through the *pampas* on the outskirts of the city and ate *bife de chorizo con chimichurri* under a willow tree. Our legs ached for days from struggling to stay upright on horses that were clearly not for beginner riders. But the unpredictability of our travels was part of the country's charm; in comparison to the States, Argentina felt wild.

The last stop on our journey was Chile. The country seemed like the holy grail of travel destinations in my mind after hearing Trey hype it up for months. And because he had studied there a couple years prior, he took the reins as our travel guide. We planned to visit both Santiago, the capital, and Valparaiso, a bohemian port city. From Mendoza, Argentina there's really only one route into Chile—a road that heads west over the Andes via the Paso de los Libertadores, one of the most scenic and dangerous passages in the world.

"I'm a little nervous about this bus ride, you guys. I don't do well with heights," I said as we waited to board the double-decker bus.

Trey placated me: "You'll be okay, the buses do this all day long, all year. They're safe. Look out the window, the view is incredible."

The bus was staffed by a skinny twenty-something Argentine who passed around free *alfajores*, two shortcake-like cookies with *dulce de leche* in the middle, an Argentine specialty. I sat down and quickly shoved two cookies in my mouth, one after the other, and washed them down with bubbly water. I offered Trey the left ear of my headphones, switched on one of my favorite albums on my iPod, and shut my eyes while we began our trip through the rugged foothills of the Andes that surrounded Mendoza's wine region. Somewhere along the journey I fell asleep, and woke up as we were passing through a tunnel under the mountains.

"Where are we?" I asked, my eyes still blurry from sleep.

"Almost at the border."

I dusted the cookie crumbs off my lap as soon as we exited the tunnel, we were treated to an astonishing snow-covered landscape. The Andes mountains hovered above us in bright white, shining like the sun that reflected off their immense and jagged peaks. Their size made them seem otherworldly, the range of mountains spread out in formations so varied and massive that it was impossible to take them all in at once.

We eventually stopped to wait with the rest of the buses and cars that joined us on the passage across the mountains and soon the driver was instructing us to get off the bus. When we descended the stairs, a cool wind whipped against my face, surprising me with the temperature change. We studied our surroundings. We were situated at the mouth of a tunnel that served as the border crossing between Argentina and Chile. We were four thousand feet above sea level, which made the air thin and the sun feel close enough to burn. After about thirty minutes waiting at the border checkpoint, where customs agents searched our belongings for contraband items like fruit, cheese, and drugs, it was our turn to pass through the rest of the immigration process. So we made our way into a large hanger where immigration officials gathered.

Passport in hand, I confidently walked up to the Chilean customs official who was clad in olive green military garb. The red, white, and blue Chilean flag sat proudly on his shoulder.

"Do we get in line?" I asked, eager to move along.

Up until that point, I was fairly confident about my Spanish language skills. I had gotten by in southern Spain during an exchange program in college and had brushed up my vocabulary working in restaurants the summer prior. I was always told that my Spanish was good, for a *gringa* at least. I was certainly not fluent, but I was proficient. The moment the Chilean officer began speaking, I remembered Trey's advice from weeks before:

"Chilean Spanish is way different; their slang is totally their own. It's tough to understand, Bree, but you'll know when you hear it."

Shit. I waved Trey over in the hopes that he would save me, but he was busy smoking a cigarette on the opposite side of the hanger. The Chilean officer continued to look at me with a mix of boredom and annoyance, then started pointing at a window across from us, where all the other passengers were lining up to pass customs. I sheepishly said, "Gracias," and slunk away. I realized it might be more difficult to communicate in Chile than I had imagined.

After more than an hour of stamping passports and exiting Argentina to enter Chile, we boarded again. The bus now smelled distinctly like a sweaty group of day-old passengers that I had apparently been nose-blind to before. We took our crumb-filled seats and prepared for the last leg of the journey. To my left sat a child I hadn't noticed before, sitting with her mother. In all of our getting to know each other, the topic of children had never come up, so I looked over at Don and asked: "Do you ever want kids?" to which he replied, "Absolutely not." "Me either," I said, and looked out the window.

Our descent began quickly. Back and forth we went, and with every turn I watched the twisting snake of a road in front of us stretch further down the mountainside. I held my breath through hairpin turns as we continued along at a speed way too fast for my comfort. We whizzed through the Aconcagua Valley, named for the river that flows downstream from the peak of the same name and creates fertile soil for the orchards of avocados and vineyards replete with Chilean grapes like Syrah, and Cabernet Sauvignon. And before I knew it we were barreling into Viña del Mar, the sister city of Valparaiso, and gathering our luggage from underneath the bus.

Rather than lodge in the more buttoned-up port city of Viña del Mar, we had booked a hostel in Valparaiso on one of the famous hills overlooking the port. We hailed the first cab that approached, threw our bags in the tiny trunk, and settled in for the final leg of the trip. I turned my face to the foggy window to take in the new view of wide streets lined with palm trees unlike any I had ever seen. Short and stout, they seemed prehistoric, like something out of a *Jurassic Park* movie.

"Where are you from?" the driver asked, not skipping a beat as we sat down. The three blondes in his backseat speaking English were clearly not locals.

"The US. We're here on vacation."

"Your Spanish is good," the driver complimented Trey, and they began a conversation about the impressive state of Chilean tourism and the places he suggested we visit while we were in town.

"Neruda," he exclaimed, one hand on the steering wheel and the other gesturing broadly at nothing in particular. "He's got a house here on Cerro Bellavista, it's a must-see."

While he and Trey shared a lively conversation, Callie and I zoned out and took in the view. We crept around the famous, sprawling downtown casino of Viña and the Pacific Ocean came into view. The only time I had seen the Pacific was on a family vacation to California in the eighth grade, and seeing it up close made me realize how far away from home I actually was. Upon the craggy shoreline, pelicans perched on the rocks and others swooped and dove in and out of the water for their next meal while seagulls barked above their heads. As we barreled down the coastal highway, we noticed what looked like an entire city built high above us along the mountainside, universities and residences overlooking the Pacific. Then another turn in the road, and another, and hills full of rainbow-colored homes like stacked Legos came into view, so vibrant against the cobalt sky and sea they looked imaginary—Valparaiso, "Valley Paradise." I barely noticed the incessant and noisy honking on the street, or the way tiny cars and buses zipped in and out of traffic like seasoned New York City cabbies.

"Which hostel?" the driver asked again, now unsure of our hostel's whereabouts.

"Caracol, in Barrio Bellavista," Trey replied. Thankfully he had been paying attention.

We swerved left, past vendors selling their wares on worn blankets laid out on the sidewalk; secondhand DVDs and books co-mingled with electronics and housewares.

"That's the market; they sell vegetables, meats, all sorts of things," our driver said as he stretched a pointed finger toward the open warehouse.

The farmer's market overflowed with peppers and avocados, citrus fruits, and deep bins of olives and spices. Packs of dogs gathered around the tiny market stalls, hoping to find someone generous enough to throw them a literal bone. Groups of people shopped and hustled around the market and nearby streets as we whizzed past.

We lurched forward, then stopped abruptly. We were hitting every single red light possible. There was no way I was about to question our driver's intentions, even though I was pretty sure we were taking the scenic route. Once we had reached the end of what appeared to be the main road, he turned sharply left and started ascending. The driver shifted into second, then third, then back down again with precision, swerving our way up the hillside along narrow streets lined with graffiti. He never flinched when we encountered another car coming directly at us from the other direction. Driving in this city was an art form, and Callie and I were both awestruck and terrified. Trey continued his conversation with the driver, wholly unaffected by the drive.

"Apaga la Tele, Viva tu Vida." "Turn off the TV, Live your life." The saying was displayed on signs propped up against windows and scrawled on t-shirts and tote bags on view as we snaked our way up Cerro Bellavista. I wondered if that was the unofficial slogan of Valpo.

Souvenirs and handmade dresses spilled out onto the cobblestone streets and tourists milled around with sensible shoes, maps in hand. Groups of young people were installed at cafe tables drinking rainbow-colored juices. No one looked like they were in a hurry. Feral dogs, more wiry and mangy than those down below, roamed or sat listlessly in the afternoon sunshine. Finally it seemed we couldn't ascend any further. "Here we are," said the driver, and threw back the e-brake.

A bright red and yellow image of a snail was painted on a sign next to the door—this must be *Hostal Caracol*. We thanked the driver and entered through a set of sturdy wooden doors, the floor creaking as we stepped into the narrow hallway.

"Hola?" we called out, hoping someone was there to check us in. After about a minute of uncertainty, a man appeared.

"Bienvenidos!" The small man, who we assumed to be the owner, wore thick-rimmed glasses and a smile and motioned for us to follow him. We passed the common area and an adjacent kitchen. We were welcome to use anything we wanted, he said, but had to make sure to replace it if it ran out. I saw only instant coffee, bread, and avocados. The kitchen opened up onto a patio where two women sat smoking and talking on white metal chairs. A large cement barbecue had been built into the wall and two empty bottles of *Carmenare* sat on its ledge next to an ashtray overflowing with butts, presumably from the night before. Beyond them was a large garden full of green potted plants with two fat palm trees on either side and I wondered how they survived rooted into the dusty desert ground. The man handed us our room keys and then

slipped away as quickly as he had come, leaving us to settle in. We threw our bags on the floor, grabbed our guidebooks and shut the door behind us, then handed the owner our passports to lock in the safe as we made our way out the door.

I had never seen a city like Valpo. During its early heyday as a center of commerce and trade in the southern hemisphere, European settlers brought with them their food, architecture, and naming conventions, but once the Panama Canal created an easier route to access the Pacific Coast, the once-bustling city began to decline. The city was made up of over forty *cerros*, hills of varying sizes, each with its own personality. Some were home to touristy hostels and restaurants, while others were filled with residences constructed of rusted metal siding or of brightly-colored houses on stilts that seemed to have acclimated themselves to the landscape. The city had a singular and complicated beauty. Though an earthquake in 1906 threatened to destroy the entire city, remnants of early opulence remained, as evidenced in the city's sturdy government buildings and ornate Victorian-style homes. Depending on where you looked, things were either falling apart or being remade into something new. Crumbling edifices were neighbors to new construction, which gave the city a feeling of metamorphosis. Valpo seemed to have no pretense, it was exactly who it said it was—the city and its inhabitants were proud of their paradise next to the sea. It felt big enough to get lost in but small enough to know intimately. As I walked the achingly steep and twisting alleys of Valpo, I felt called to uncover something new about myself. Exactly what that was, I wasn't yet sure.

We tried to take in as much as we could during our two day stay, popping in and out of cafes, alternating between the ubiquitous fresh juices and cheap beer on offer. The three of us had settled into a groove as travel companions, and while there was still lingering tension between Trey and Callie, for the most part we enjoyed each other's company. We ate avocado on *marraqueta*, a staple Chilean bread said to have been created by the french settlers of Valparaiso. We sat overlooking the ocean and stuffed ourselves with seafood *empanadas* oozing with cheese. We visited an old prison that had been made into an art installation by local artists, its walls made of used wine bottles set into concrete to catch the sunlight. Every surface there was full of bright graffiti: a woman with long dark hair surrounded by pink birds, a man dressed in a rainbow-colored bunny suit. Tires were repurposed and painted in vibrant reds and yellows and a children's playground was constructed of pipe and metal tubes. Everything was refashioned and made beautiful, painted and redone from something old, or worn down, or broken, into something colorful and new—transformation was at the center of everything.

Part of me felt ready to stop moving, but we still had one more place to see before Trey departed: Santiago, Chile's capital city. Getting there from the coast was a quick ninety-minute bus trip through the Casablanca Valley, which was a far cry from the day long bus rides of our previous travels. As our bus left the station, meandering through the busy streets, I vowed to return to Valpo.

Trey, who was no stranger to the landscape, had his face buried in a book while Callie and I watched the terrain turn from coastal to the farmland of the central valley. And as we continued east, the mountain range which runs parallel to the Andes came into view. I watched the peaks making slow shadows on the fertile valley below. Sweeping fields of lush greenery, avocado trees, and vineyards spread as far as the eye could see. I shifted in my seat, peered out the window and noticed a donkey hitched to a signpost on the side of the road. Everywhere my eyes landed looked like the vast, quiet, middle of nowhere. But before I knew it, the landscape changed again. The highway now cut through the mountain range, with hills of dirt and dust and patches of green on either side of us. We passed through a four-lane tunnel and on the other side met the outskirts of Santiago.

"What is that? It looks like a fire." I pointed ahead to a cloudy gray mass in the sky.

"We're almost there, that's the smog. When we're there we won't notice it," Trey said, poking his nose out from his book. "The city is always shrouded in smog like this—even worse in the winter, trust me."

The bus barreled into the streets of downtown Santiago, the *centro*, which were busy and loud in contrast to the unhurried pace of the beach towns we had come from.

"That's the presidential palace," Trey explained, as we passed a few gray government buildings. "You know, the US helped Pinochet and his guys bomb that in 1973. It was September 11th, actually. You know us, always the interventionists."

"That's crazy. How long did the dictatorship last?" Callie asked.

"Until 1989."

I imagined what life was like in 1989 and looked out the window.

We had planned to meet up with Pedro, a brother of a classmate Trey had befriended while finishing up his coursework in Santiago a couple years before. Trey promised Pedro would be a top-notch tour guide. On Trey and Pedro's advice, we were staying in a neighborhood called Barrio Lastarria. It was located adjacent a hill named Cerro Santa Lucía which was originally occupied by the people indigenous to Chile but then conquered and renamed by the Spanish. The ornate castle and its elaborate structures still stood and offered one of the best views of the city.

We only had a few days to experience as much as we could of Santiago, so as soon as we had showered off our bus trip, we immediately set out on foot to our first destination, a hip bar named *La Catedral* to people-watch over drinks. Trey led us up a set of stairs and I held my hand on his back so I wouldn't lose him in the crowd of people that only got denser as we made our way back toward the bar. Packs of cigarettes with bold warnings on their labels littered the tables. Music blared on the speakers and willed me to dance, find a drink, get loud. I relished the feeling of letting lose, the adrenaline at the beginning of an evening when I had no idea where the night would take me. The city was the perfect backdrop to feel young and alive and brand new. Santiago pulsed with energy, a city developing into itself. Once we had found a spot to claim on the balcony of the third floor, Trey shot up out of his seat. "*Pedro, amigo! Como estai?*" he screamed over the blaring *reggaetón* at the sight of his old friend.

I looked left to find Pedro, who was short and solid with lush black hair cut military-style.

"*Amigo!* It's been too long!" said Trey.

"I'm Pedro, nice to meet you!" Pedro said after he had made his way to us. He turned to Callie and me with a mischievous smile on his face and gave us each a kiss on the cheek. I liked him immediately.

The next two days Trey and Pedro reminisced about old times as the four of us traipsed through the city visiting Trey's old haunts. We hiked up Cerro San Cristobal, one of the largest green spaces in the city, and meandered around market stalls of artisans selling brightly-colored textiles and jewelry made of lapiz lazuli in Barrio Bellavista. We climbed to the top of Cerro Santa Lucía to admire the view of the city and the Andes that were only slightly visible through the smog. Pedro bought us all a sugary-sweet drink of peaches and husked wheat called *mote con huesillo* on a street corner after we had stuffed ourselves full of steak sandwiches and draft beer. We were all happy, including and maybe most of all, Trey. I imagined him two years before during that wet July, bundled up in his woolen pea coat and hungover, searching for something he wasn't sure he'd ever find. He looked content now, running through the summer streets of Santiago again, and I felt satisfaction that part of his newfound happiness was because of me.

Trey left South America a week later to head back to the farm and the short days of December in Pennsylvania. It was easier than the first time we had parted, but after only a few days the email communication turned sour and I started to worry about him and about managing the long distance. I had finally told my parents about our engagement and they responded as anticipated, with both thinly veiled anger and disapproval at my choice. There were no congratulations and no excitement on the other side of the line. I was hurt and angry but tried to hide my disappointment so at least one of us could enjoy our good news. Their reaction served to further distance me from them and without their support, I leaned on Trey.

But my travel with Callie continued, despite my focus on other things. We went to Salta in the north of Argentina to visit the salt flats of *Purmamarca*. We shared coca leaves with two Argentine women who took silly pictures of us with distorted camera views and I bought a sweater with little brown alpacas spread across the chest to commemorate the trip. I hadn't heard from Trey for over a day when I checked my email for the first time in a red-carpeted internet cafe in the middle of town. We had been busy roaming around the colonial cathedrals and enjoying the view from a gondola that swung us up the green side of a mountain. The bold lettering caught my eye as it always did when I clicked open my email, but I read too quickly for my mind to process, something about a suspected DUI. Then there were many emails, back to back, all written as his stream of consciousness again.

January 3, 2009 - 12:18 pm
Yep. DUI. Remember nothing. Took a pill from some guy I was talking to at the bar. Who knows. Just tell me you can't deal with this shit so I can cease to exist.

RIP THEM UP BY THE ROOTS

February, 2009

"You've gotta wet the soil first, then press the seed into it." Trey dunked the entire seedling tray into the potting soil, then ran his hand over the top of it to get rid of the excess. It had never crossed my mind how plants were grown from seed. He had done this countless times before, but I was learning.

"Let's finish all of these flats of tomatoes then we can take a break," he said.

"Okay, cool. Is this right?" I replied, trying my hardest not to mess anything up. The farm was now both of our livelihoods. My lack of farming experience was less important than my desire to be with him, so I tried my best to learn quickly and, at the very least, to stay out of the way. For now, the off-season farm work consisted of planting seeds in trays in a heated greenhouse and ordering supplies off the internet. Soon enough we'd be schlepping our harvest to farmer's markets. Though he had described the work as "intense," I had no idea what kind of labor was to come.

Callie and I had cut the rest of our trip short since I had officially run out of money and my priority was getting home to Trey. His parents had temporarily left the farm, leaving Trey in charge, and it was the first time they had given him the reins to manage the property alone. Despite his DUI, the new opportunity seemed to course-correct his mood and with an entire farm at his disposal, Trey was ambitious about getting us from the farm to the next step in our journey. Over a number of lengthy drunken conversations between the two of us, we decided that we would follow through with our plan and leave the country after the farm season finished—he had always wanted to build a house with his own hands and he had finally found someone who was willing to do it with him. He was ready to run and I was ready to follow. What was also true but went unsaid was that we would go somewhere the debt collectors couldn't find him, where my parent's divorce didn't exist, where Trey's legions of past-lovers didn't threaten my self-esteem, and where there was no one to know but each other. We planned to leave the following November, with as much money as we could possibly save up. We hadn't decided where we would land but we'd figure that out soon enough.

He had gotten a position as a manager of a farm internship program up the mountain from our house to pay the bills during the lean winter months, and some of the workers who had signed up for the program needed housing, so we decided to open up our home to roommates. The plan was to give a spot in the house to anyone who needed it in exchange for work on our own farm, since we had three rooms and an empty attic. That way, participants could be close to the program and we could take advantage of extra hands during the farm prepping time of the year. Over pizza one night, Trey mentioned that he had found the first person interested in our little farmer housing program, a man from the Dominican Republic named Elias.

"He and his brother, Carlos, are going to swing by in a few days to meet us if that's okay," he told me.

"Of course, what kind of farming do they want to do?" I asked.

"Flowers for Elias, I think—he'll be able to help you out with those. His brother wants to raise livestock." Trey folded his greasy pizza slice in two while I dabbed at mine with a napkin.

"Sounds good, and Elias wants to move in here?"

"Yup, next week," he answered. Apparently only Elias needed housing, I was later told that he had moved back to the area as a last resort after his career as a dancer in New York City had ended.

"No problem," I said, of course.

On the day of our first meeting, I cleaned our place as much as I could, scrubbing the floors and dusting in between the railings of the old wooden staircase. I wanted it to seem like we were prepared and professional despite the fact that I felt anything but. My mother had taught me, though she never articulated it outright, that a spotless house was the key to looking and feeling like everything was under control.

At 6 PM we heard a tap at the back door and opened it to find two men standing on our patio.

The brothers could not have looked more different. Carlos stood about 6' 5" and seemed as though he had been hefting huge weight above his shoulders his entire life, while Elias was lithe, wore a sparkly purple turban on his head, and looked like a dancer. Carlos started in English while Elias, positioned two steps behind him, squinted his eyes with focus.

"Hey guys! I'm Carlos."

"I'm Briana. Trey's fiancé. Nice to meet you."

"This is my brother Elias," he said, placing his hand on Elias's shoulder. "He's going to be helping on the farm too."

Elias stepped forward and stretched his hand out to shake—his nails were glossy and perfectly-filed. "Hi. Nice to meet you," he said slowly, as if he considered every word before it left his mouth. "No hablo mucho ingles," *I don't know much English*, he continued. Dominican Spanish was different—his words had round edges.

"We speak Spanish, we'd love to practice with you," Trey interjected, so we continued in Spanish, hoping to accommodate our new housemate.

The four of us made our way into the carpeted living room where there were no cigarette butts or half-empty wine bottles in sight, then filed upstairs into the skinny hallway that barely held the four of us.

"Here's your room," Trey said, pointing to the tiny room. It was painted dark blue with two large windows that splashed sunlight on the walls and gave the room a cheerier feel than the others. "It's small but you could put a mattress on the floor and there's space for your things."

Elias slowly made his way out from behind us. "Thank you," he replied. A smile crept onto his face, but he was quiet. He looked out the window at the fire station next door, then back at us.

"Okay, great. Elias can move in next week," Carlos decided.

After a few more minutes of small talk we started making our way to the kitchen to say goodbye when Japhy lumbered nervously out from his normal spot in the living room, his ears were back and his tail was wedged between his legs. I had never known a dog with anxiety like Japhy, he was constantly nervous.

"Oh! Hellooooo my friend!" Elias said, so animated at the sight of Japhy that he practically leapt into the air. He immediately knelt beside him and stroked his soft black head.

"That's Japhy, he lives here too. He's a good boy, just a little strange," Trey explained.

I bent down to join Elias who was now holding Japhy's boxy head between his hands and rubbing his ears vigorously. "Good boy!" he squealed over and over, and I couldn't help but like him and simultaneously wonder why he was applying to a farming program in the Pennsylvania suburbs. Elias seemed better suited for something more extravagant and less dirty. Japhy relished the attention, wagging his tail so hard his body looked like it was about to split in two. We said goodbye and the following week Elias moved into the blue room upstairs. He carried only a few items with him, nothing that wouldn't fit inside a small cardboard box.

We got two more roommates the following month, a young guy named John and a friend of his whose name I'll never remember. John looked the part of a wannabe farmer with beat-up jeans and dirt beneath his fingernails. I wasn't sure if or where he showered, since he never seemed to use ours. John would write lengthy love letters to his girlfriend out of state and when he wasn't working the farm with us, he kept to himself in his room. His friend was so quiet that Trey and I wondered if she said more than five words the entire month she lived with us. She crept around silently to her tiny room in the attic and down to the basement where she and John kept their kimchi; the sulfur smell rose up through the floorboards.

In the back of our minds, escape to another country always loomed, like a zip cord we could pull to release ourselves from our current state, taking us to a supposed safety net. To me, the closer we came to our departure, the scarier the idea of the move became. Trey, on the other hand, had enough excitement about the trip for both of us. In theory, I longed for another adventure, but in practice, I wasn't sure if I had the bravery to follow through with our lofty plans. On days when I couldn't fathom the work that awaited us on the other side of our move, I buried myself in tasks. Distraction was easy to come by on the farm. By March, however, we still hadn't decided which country we would move to, even though the question came up in conversation almost every night.

"Mexico is perfect, you'd like Oaxaca or Chiapas. Tons of culture," he'd say. He preferred Mexico to the other spots on our short list.

"But the drugs, Trey, it's dangerous right now. I don't know," I'd reply.

"It's close though. Closer than anywhere else we're thinking about." He knew what to say to sway me.

"What about Chile? I loved it there. Stable economy, safe. Plenty of work for foreigners. We could easily teach English," I offered. "I did some research last night online. There are like, ten English-teaching institutes in Santiago."

"You're not wrong, and I obviously like it there. There's plenty of the country I haven't seen."

Most nights we'd stop after we wandered into this decision-making territory, but that night I continued, feeling we needed it to be settled. The anxiety of the unknown was slowly getting to me.

I pressed, "Honestly, I don't want to move to Mexico. If we're going to do this, I want to seriously think about Chile. It makes the most sense out of everywhere. Costa Rica is full of Americans, too many surfers, and there's no way we could afford land there."

"You're right. I get it. I love Mexico and would love to see Costa Rica, but I get it. Chile it is."

"Seriously? You're good with it?"

"Yes, anywhere that's not here."

And that was that—we were moving to Chile.

"We're going to have to bust our asses this summer to afford land there," he continued. "We can do it, but full-time farm work is tough, backbreaking. Not like the prep work we've been doing. And we're going to have to fill all the greenhouse and all the fields, do something totally different from what any other farmers are offering. That's how we'll make the most money. We'll need at least thirty thousand dollars in cash. Not sure how we'll get it down there though. Maybe we stuff it in our shoes."

I realized he wasn't exaggerating about any of it, not even the shoes. We had less than a year to save enough money to start our lives over in Chile, but Trey wasn't phased by our timeline. He had everything—the crops, the markets, the finances, the move—all planned out in his head; the only thing left to do was the work. Problem was, I had never worked a day of back-breaking anything in my life.

Hilltop Farm sat back about a quarter mile from the road, up a straight and narrow driveway. His parents had purchased the land in the late 1980's, built the pretty white farmhouse, and named their property after the prime view the location afforded them of the surrounding forested hills. The house was flanked by greenhouses on either side, four in total, all draped in thick plastic and a good twenty degrees hotter than the outside temperature at any given time of the year. His family had named each greenhouse for its contents or the person who had built it: the one they'd lovingly named "Brother" after Trey; the "Other One" where vegetables grew; the "Mama" held flowers; and the "Little Pisser" was the house for the starter plants. An acre of blueberry fields grew behind the house and led up to the top field where pigs usually roamed in their own enclosed, muddy playground. His parents owned all the land up to the fence row and another fertile acre that went unused, to the far west of the house.

Before long, the winter finally started to loosen its grip on us. In the afternoons I noticed how the daylight stretched differently through the windows of the gray house, and on the farm the signs of spring were starting to show. The seeds we had tended in the winter had turned into thriving little plants and soon I had learned enough about farming to make myself useful. Tomatoes shot their tiny green leaves up through the soil of the seedling trays, two or three at a time. Carrots, zinnias, snapdragons all came up from seed. Trey chose one sprout to keep and yanked the others up from their roots. I wasn't sure how he decided which one deserved to grow. "Thinning," he called it. And the flower-growing operation was left almost entirely to me.

Trey's mom had been growing flowers at the farm long enough to accumulate a cult following and a nickname. "The flower lady," her legions of fans lovingly called her, and I hoped I would be half as good as she was. Eventually the bright magenta peonies sprang open from their dormant flower beds and I called her to tell her the good news. "Cut them and wrap them in newspaper, then save them in the walk-in cooler. They'll last longer that way," she said. She assured me our farmer's market customers would love them. Next, the hydrangeas showed their green buds around the perennial flower beds, snapdragons, Queen Anne's lace, butterfly bushes—everything that had been lying dormant sprang back to life in the course of a few weeks.

But at home, the roommates were getting restless. Odd jobs and off-season farm work didn't provide enough money to go around, and Trey's plan to give the live-in farm hands additional work at the farm up the hill kept being delayed due to the program's lack of funds.

"I'll keep helping but what do we do if they don't give us jobs?" asked Elias one day, as the two of us sat together on a patch of dirt outside a greenhouse watching Trey hammer posts into the finally-thawed ground. Sometimes I caught myself staring at him while he worked, amazed at how capable he was.

I flicked two cigarettes out of my pack, passed Elias one, and lit my own.

"I have no idea. But you can stay with us as long as you'd like," I said.

His gaze shifted to Trey, then back at me. Japhy limped over, his bad knees were acting up again, which meant there must be rain in the forecast.

"I love you Japhy, do you love me?!" Elias exclaimed in English. Japhy looked un-amused.

Trey lit his own cigarette and sauntered over. "Hey guys, let's till this bed up, we're planting green beans and artichokes over here next week and the soil needs work."

"*Ayúdame,*" Elias said with an outstretched hand. He was so slight I nearly threw him when I tugged him upright. I wondered how long he could hold on without a steady paycheck. I stomped out my cigarette in the mud below my feet, brushed off my jeans and we both followed Trey down to the greenhouse.

It was June before we knew it and the rains came heavy that year, dark and gloomy days, one after another, which flooded the fields daily. Farming is so dependent on uncontrollable things like the sun and rain, or the whims of animals. We did what we could with what we were given but neither of us was good at accepting the things we couldn't control.

A call came on a Monday from Trey's parents. His father asked if we would be interested in living on the farm rent-free for the remainder of the year to care for the farmhouse.

"Thanks Dad, we've got our place leased through the end of the month, then we can make the move," Trey said calmly through the line and hung up.

"So, what are we going to do with the roommates? They obviously can't live on the farm with us, there's not enough room."

"The county isn't coming through with any money, it's only a matter of time until this whole farming internship project falls apart, and we can't afford to keep them on ourselves." I was taken aback at how easy it was for him to dismiss the people who had become our friends.

"I feel bad for them. I wish we could help and I know how much you wanted the farming program to work out."

"It is what it is Bree. I don't know much but I know how to farm. I know how to do this. I've been farming my entire life. We will be fine," he assured me.

Trey gave Elias and the others the news and everyone vacated the house the following week. I never found out where they ended up. Cutting ties that way made me deeply uncomfortable, but I was starting to realize that unlike me, Trey's priority was not the comfort of others.

We said goodbye to our gray house and I followed him to the farm where he had grown up, about five miles away from my childhood home. We owned so few things there wasn't even a need for movers and his books took up the majority of the moving boxes. A sense of growing worry crept over me in the moments I was still, which were few now that the farm season had begun. So I kept my mind busy and my glass full.

WEDDING DRESS
June, 2009

My mom asked me to go shopping with her for my wedding dress. I had never been the kind of girl who had dreamed of an elaborate wedding, and all the attention showered on brides seemed embarrassing to me at the time. But I still needed a dress. So I invited my childhood best friend, Kristen, and her mother, Faye, the only other motherly figure in my life, along for the trip. I figured it would be a nice way to spend time with everyone since our relationships had felt strained since I came back from Argentina engaged to a man my family and friends barely knew. Since my return, I'd spent most, if not all, of my time with Trey. I desperately wanted an afternoon away from farm work and I hoped I could smooth over any negative feelings my mom had toward my pending marriage with a special wedding-related outing.

So we all took the day off work and piled into my mom's green sedan. The questions commenced immediately.

"Tell us all about your new man. I can't believe you're getting married, sweetie!" Faye offered, sounding genuinely excited.

"He's great. I can't believe it either. He's a farmer but has his master's in foreign policy from Georgetown." I always made sure to add that last bit in, lest anyone think Trey was one-dimensional.

My mom stayed quiet with her eyes fixed on the road.

"And your mom tells me you two want to move to Chile? Wow, so you want to go back to South America. For how long? What do you want to do there?" My mom had obviously filled her in—well, at least it proved she was actually listening.

"Well yeah, we're not sure when we want to leave yet, but we want to go there and build a house. The economy isn't great here right now and I've always wanted to live abroad." I felt like a robot reciting a script, and I wasn't prepared to divulge the actual timeline to them, not like this anyway.

"So, you're going to leave again?" Kristen's voice held a tinge of annoyance, or sadness. I couldn't tell.

"I'll miss everyone, too." I tried to change the subject, but my mom wasn't going to let the moment go without speaking up.

"I don't think this is a good idea. You barely know this man—what's the rush? Why can't you just wait until next year and we can all get to know him and spend more time together? I don't like the idea of you leaving again and moving five thousand miles away."

Even though she had been the one to suggest wedding dress shopping, she had to have one last shot at dissuading me from marrying him. I had heard this argument before but I had already made my decision. I had chosen Trey and he had chosen me, which was an even bigger miracle. I wanted to be taken seriously, but I wasn't going to resolve our issues on the car ride to the bridal boutique. What I really wanted to say was: *Why are you still living with dad after everything?* And, *You're miserable. Who are you to tell me what to do?* Our judgments of one another were loud, even in the silence.

The four of us arrived at the shop without the usual fanfare and giddy chatter of brides and their mothers. I tried to hide my disappointment with a fake smile plastered on my face. After today, I thought, I wouldn't have to entertain their questions if I didn't want to. We'd be married in October and were leaving almost immediately after that.

"Welcome to Anne Bailey Bridal!" the cheery saleswoman chirped. "What are we looking for today, ladies?" I wondered if she could tell we weren't the happiest group she'd ever seen come into the shop.

"I'm getting married in a few months. I have an idea of what I want: empire waist, cap sleeves. Romantic," I said, hoping the dress specifics would offset the quiet entrance.

"Oh lovely, I have a dress you'd love. It sounds exactly like what you're looking for."

She floated into an adjacent room full of puffy white gowns and shuffled through the stack before landing on the dress—she snatched it out of the mix like a ripe piece of fruit, the prized one of the bunch. And it was perfect. Slight intricate beading on tiny tulle sleeves, empire waist, just like I had imagined. Best of all, it fit me like a glove, like it was made for me. Everyone oohed and ahhed when I slipped it on and despite the earlier tension, I felt like someone's bride.

"It fits you perfectly, there's barely a need to tailor it," the saleswoman said as she poked and prodded, lifting and pulling the train out behind me to show the dress in its full glory. I flipped over the price tag. $1,200. I hoped that wouldn't be a problem.

"Mom I love it, this is it," I insisted, even though she knew.

"It does fit you well, it's very pretty. If you're sure this is what you want," my mother said. But I wasn't sure she was talking about the dress.

The rest of the afternoon went smoothly. The earlier tension had dissipated and by the time we all returned to the farm I was feeling hopeful about introducing Trey to Kristen and Faye. Our car pulled into the driveway. As Kristen and I jumped out into the sunshine, I noticed him standing in the garage, not ten feet in front of us, focused on scrubbing something I couldn't see. He didn't look up.

"Hey there," I said sweetly to him. "I want to introduce you to my other family. This is my best friend, Kristen—I've told you all about her—and her mom, Faye."

He continued to clean, his gaze never shifting from the stainless steel tub in front of him.

"I thought you could meet everyone, since they're all here. I know you're busy…"

He didn't move an inch to acknowledge us. It felt like a dark cloud had descended.

I didn't want to believe what was happening, that he was ignoring us on purpose.

"No big deal, it's just your mother-in-law," my mom said under her breath, but loud enough for all to hear.

He finally turned toward us—his weighty boots smacking the pavement as though to prove the point that work was the priority—and coolly said, "Hello." Then he pounded off, leaving us speechless, standing in the hot driveway. We had inconvenienced him and he had shown a side of himself that was unconcerned with looks and happy first impressions.

Instead of hearing the concerns my friends and family expressed after that day, I constructed walls that could protect me from their opinions.

LITTLE FARMER
June, 2009

Summer eventually came, as Pennsylvania summers do, with humid mornings and nights full of lightning bugs. We were in love and that colored my days with a rosiness that allowed me to focus on the positive and ignore everything else, like Trey's growing surliness. My tendency toward being relentlessly optimistic served me well.

I remember the basil and tomato sandwiches he would hand deliver to me in our bedroom while we listened to summer thunderstorms. Or skimming through guidebooks to research neighborhoods in Santiago, discussing Henry Miller and Big Sur and California in the '60s. Our shared desire to escape bonded us and more than anything, we hoped Chile would be our chance to live a life we designed from scratch.

After we had installed ourselves in the farm full time, any separation between work and life fell away. Work was life and life was work. Trey was in his element and I did my best to keep up. He had note cards full of to-do lists strewn over every surface, as were bundles of seed packets: tomatillos, heirloom tomatoes, purple carrots. Every waking moment was spent planning and organizing and working—what to plant here, what to sow there—as he coordinated crops like a choreographer. The intricacies of the job amazed me. The amount of knowledge one had to possess was something to be learned in a lifetime, not over a season. Every

Saturday we traveled to Philadelphia, a quick hour and a half drive from the farm, to hawk our veggies and flowers at a farmer's market in a swanky neighborhood downtown called Rittenhouse Square. Every Sunday we would work our second market of the week, much smaller but just as busy, in the town where we both grew up. Each week prepping for the markets took three full days of near-constant labor from sunup until past sundown.

The markets were grueling, but to me they were also incredibly fun. Trey loved the hard work but hated the small talk, whereas I loved the socializing and tolerated the work it took to get there. We were like two different sides of the same coin. I was especially quick to share our homesteading dream with our customers and in turn, they were happy to support our moving-to-Chile-fund. Our farming business was profitable. We were lucky, too—it was right before the artisan farming and hustle economy boom of the early 2010s that brought all sorts of hipsters out of the woodwork and back to the land. Before fermented foods were hip, before kombucha was mainstream, before food trucks were everywhere and local food was a buzzword, farming was fringe and we were in it.

Veggie production was ramping up and despite the incessant rain earlier in the season, the crops were growing right on schedule. Every day I'd learn something new about farming. He taught me about the different varieties of plants and veggies and why it mattered where seeds came from. We focused on heirloom varieties like green zebra tomatoes, herbs I'd never heard of, and cucumbers that looked like lemons or baby watermelons. We grew greenhouses full of salad greens, bok choi, tat soi, varieties of spinach and lettuce, hearty and fragile, spicy and sweet, then topped the mix with dainty edible flowers, which our market customers loved. Harvesting the greens was painstaking work and he had learned the best methods from the Mexican farm workers he shared fields with in California in his early twenties, though he said they were better and faster than he could ever be. He taught me how to install drip tape to water the needy little plants during the hot summer days; the black plastic snaked around their roots and delivered hydration in measured drops with the turn of a spigot. Once the tomatoes came on, later in the growing season, he showed me how to pick those by squeezing in between the tall wire tomato cages. "They'll stain your hands," he said, "but you can eat the cherry ones while you do it." I loved the sun golds, ripened and warmed by the sun, sweet like dessert. Whenever I thought I had picked the plants clean, I'd double back to check if I could find a few more. All I had to do was shift my point of view and there they were, dozens more, revealing themselves with my change in perspective. Running the farm was incredibly physical work. With so much cutting, pruning, digging, tilling, hauling, and maneuvering, even my spry twenty-three-year-old back ached at the end of the day.

While Trey managed the majority of the farm work, the flower growing was up to me. Trey's mother came to visit to show me where the rest of the perennials would come up around the farm and how to properly bouquet. I felt clumsy at first, holding all the stems at once was hard, but with practice I grew capable. Most of all, I was happy to contribute in a way that was my own. And the animals, like the veggies and flowers, were happy and thriving. We made a makeshift chicken rooster in the shed next to the Little Pisser to house baby chicks. One hundred of the best breed of meat birds came in a cardboard box in the mail and I learned that chickens weren't sold like puppies in a pet store. To add to the mix, we bought fifty quail and ten pheasants, then gave each group their own space in which to roam. And because Trey said that farm-raised pork would always be in high demand, we bought six piglets from a farm in central Pennsylvania to round out our animal offerings. We named all six of them, but Floppy McFlopperson (who had one ear doubled over like a page in a book), Roy, and Big Bertha were my favorites. It was my job to feed them, so every morning I'd walk up the hill to their pen, past the zinnias and blueberry bushes, and they'd squeal and run in circles until I gave them their breakfast. If they were lucky, I'd sneak them leftovers from the night before. They stuck their snouts through the metal fencing and I'd rub their fuzzy pink faces while I sipped my morning coffee. They grew fast and before I knew it, they were all much larger than I was.

Every morning, Trey woke up at the crack of dawn. I watched him out the window from our warm bed, lighting his first cigarette, black coffee in hand, trudging through the still-barren blueberry fields, his boots leaving outlines in the damp grass. After I gave myself enough guilt to get up and out of bed, I crept downstairs to make my usual breakfast of toast with peanut butter and coffee. I threw on his black plastic gardening clogs since I had none of my own and couldn't be bothered to tie anything, not that early.

"Trey!" I called into the quiet. His boot tracks had now disappeared with the sunlight's arrival. He was either in one of the greenhouses or in the far field, scribbling away on note cards or planting something.

No answer.

Damn, I'd have to go find him.

"Trey!" I yelled louder, throwing my voice as far as I could. I was sure I'd wake the neighbors, but thankfully, they were at least an acre away.

"Come on Japhy," I said, and yanked the broken patio door open. If I had to make the small pilgrimage down to the far field, at least I'd have company.

As soon as Japhy and I got closer to the Brother greenhouse, his obscured figure came into focus. He was weeding. He was meticulous about everything but weeding most of all—he had the precision of an engineer, no errant growth was safe. He took pride in focusing on the details.

"Hey! I've been calling for you!" I said at normal volume.

Still nothing.

"Dude!" I shouted, which finally got his attention. I noticed the headphone cords dangling around his neck.

"Hey sorry, had my music up loud," he said.

"Yeah, no worries. Want some help? You hungry?" I asked.

"Eh, I'm good. Gotta finish these rows before it gets too hot to be in here. I'll come up later," he replied.

"Alright, anything for me to work on?" I knew full well there was enough work for twenty extra hands, let alone two.

"Yeah. You can start to till the back beds behind the Mama greenhouse, where you can plant more flowers. We've gotta start squirreling this money away, little farmer," he replied.

"Sounds great, handsome." I bounced toward him over the seeded rows as nimbly as I could, careful not to step on the growing arugula and spinach. "Hi there," I said as I reached him. "I love you." I leaned in and looked him straight in the eye, which felt more intimate than I was used to, at least this sober. "See you in a minute."

My relationship with Trey was evolving. I began to see him, consciously or not, as a tutor. I watched intently as he turned fallow land into money and devised intricate systems to provide for the whole lot of vegetables, flowers and animals we had invited onto the farm. I had never seen anyone care so deeply about anything before and it inspired me to find something I loved that much. In the absence of my own passion, I passionately loved him.

I shuffled back up to the house and carried my journal from the window bay to the kitchen table to make my list for the day. Historically, I had never been the organized type. In school, I would buy fancy agendas only to have them sit, unused, at the bottom of my backpack. List-making made more sense to me because it could be tackled one day at a time, which was way less intimidating than an entire month laid out before me. Sometimes I'd write down something I'd already completed just for the pleasure of crossing it off. I flipped the page over and looked at the new month. Summer was here—it had come fast. Our wedding was less than six months away and I hadn't started planning. Because our life and lifestyle revolved around farming, there was little time for anything that wasn't profitable or farming-related, so planning our wedding was not high on the list of priorities.

Affection wasn't high on the list of priorities either, at least not for him. I sought it every chance I could get. I'd catch him in the walk-in cooler, or the seeding greenhouse, and loop my arms around his. Once, Paul Simon was playing on the Bose speaker, just loud enough to hear.

"I love this song," I said, as the first few notes of *Peace Like a River* started. *Long past the midnight curfew we sat starry-eyed.*

"It reminds me of Santiago, and the Rio Mapocho," he said.

He pulled me close, hoisted me on top of the metal table, then kissed me. *This song will always remind me of you*, I thought.

"Alright, I'll be down at the Brother," he said, and the moment was over as soon as it had started.

At the end of each day we'd run outside to close the greenhouses against the deer and bunnies and whatever else was bound to prowl the farm at night. I felt the grass between my toes, the ground beneath my feet, the air was still humid and everything smelled of wet grass and earth. On the farm I knew my job and the importance of it. He'd look my way or I'd look his, smiling, and in that moment I was very sure that my life was headed in the right direction.

THE SUNSHINE CLUB

July, 2009

Trey and I weren't alone in our pursuit of a different kind of life. He had an entire community of people he had met throughout his tenure as a farm kid and if there was one thing I was good at, it was making friends. Our motley group was a mix of work-a-days turned entrepreneurs, like Sam, a bus driver and Trappist monk turned cheese monger. Or Noah, an engineer turned butcher and meat farmer. Will the pro-cyclist turned baker rounded out our little circle. It seemed as if the work attracted people looking to start over.

We bonded over a shared understanding of the difficulties of running your own small food business. The money fluctuated constantly, things out of your control could easily derail you, and the work was constant. But our work offered something that conventional jobs didn't: freedom. Freedom to pursue what excited us on any given day, freedom to create something from nothing, and freedom to share the thing we'd made with other people. Those are the freedoms you'd share openly and proudly with others when they asked you how you liked running a farm business. But the biggest freedom? That was the fact that you answered to no one but yourself. Not one of us would have traded in those freedoms for a bigger paycheck. "Working stiffs be damned" could have been our motto.

By July we were thick as thieves. After our local farmer's market concluded every Sunday, we'd convene on our farm for a weekly get together we soon dubbed The Sunshine Club, in part because of the nickname one of the farmers had given me, Little Miss Sunshine. After the long weekend we all had just enough goods left to barter and trade with one another. Greens for cheese. Tomatoes for beef. Flowers for bread. Who brought the beers was a matter of shifting responsibility. Our buddy Josh, a local chef, usually tagged along to help Trey cook up the main meal of the get-together and our weekly meetings ran late into the night until we could barely keep our eyes open.

It was the last Sunday in July, a few days before my twenty-fourth birthday. I had beat Trey home from the market. Our friends would soon arrive but I sat by myself on the back porch and stared out at the blueberry bushes in silence. The birds chirped at one another from above my head while a butterfly perched on the ivy that crawled up the wall of the screened-in porch. It wasn't often I had time alone with my thoughts. In fact, I usually avoided moments like these for a reason. My mind wandered.

This is my favorite place in the world, I thought, *and in a few months we'll be gone.* The thought rattled around my head for a minute until I heard the clank of keys on the table, Trey's boots on the kitchen floor.

"Hey there, little farmer," he said playfully, as he burst through the sliding back door with beers in hand. They clinked in their flimsy six-pack cases as he set them down on the long glass table that was the central hub of our gatherings. "Josh just got here." Let the party begin.

Eventually the rest of the group arrived and through the music I could hear their muffled voices in the kitchen, something about pork belly and the cuts of meat that Noah had brought. Will and Trey joined me on the porch while the others stayed inside.

"This stuff is great, Will," Trey said, voraciously biting a crust of bread.

"Goes well with your tomatoes," Will returned.

I shook a beer out of its wet case and opened it with the bottom of a Bic lighter and a flick of my wrist—a party trick Trey had taught me the summer before.

"Damn Bree—nicely done! Open mine, will ya?" Noah said, lumbering onto the patio and into the conversation. Noah was 6' 5" and 300 lbs, and the energy he brought with him was just as big as he was.

I easily opened his beer, gave him a wink, and felt a burst of cool-girl satisfaction.

Then Josh appeared, half in the bag. "Got about ten minutes till the soup's ready. Have this for now," he said as he placed an overflowing bowl of our greens down in the center of the table, edible red and yellow marigolds decorating the top.

"I picked these up at our Staten Island market," Sam said of his contribution: a skinny bottle of fancy balsamic vinegar and two delicate flower-wrapped goat cheeses to share.

Eventually we carried bowls and platters and bottles of red wine to the table from inside and I noticed it suddenly felt much cooler out. The days were still hot and long, but fall was coming. Japhy loped out the door and installed himself at my feet since he knew I was the most likely to gift him secret scraps straight from the table.

"Let's eat!" Noah said, and a few of us clinked our beer bottles while a happy song played in the background.

My mind wandered again without my consent, and I felt the peculiar fear of knowing a truth you wish were not true. How can you miss a place you haven't left yet?

I don't want to leave, I thought.

But I knew I would follow him anywhere. We bought our tickets to Chile and took the rest of the money we had saved up—which amounted to around $20,000—to the bank to turn into hundred dollar bills.

IT LOOKED BEAUTIFUL

October, 2009

"Do you even want to do this?" I asked. I had found him outside rearranging drip tape, and when he saw me, standing in my favorite red dress in the driveway, he continued to stomp back and forth from the seeding greenhouse to the garage, back and forth over and over, as if I were invisible. Eventually he got so agitated that he threw down the drip tape and jumped in the truck so I jumped in too, then he slammed the door behind him.

"Do you even want to do this?" I asked again. "This is supposed to be a special night; it's our rehearsal dinner."

"Of course I do," he said, taking a cigarette from the pack he kept in his glove compartment. He still hadn't looked at me. So I looked out the window as we drove down to the Farmhouse, where we would get married the following day. The leaves on the maple trees that lined the winding road leading into town were turning color already. It was the most beautiful fall I could remember.

That night we had a large dinner party at the farm during which Trey and I forgave each other and we all drank too much.

The day of our wedding I woke up with an intense hangover and a pounding between my eyes so loud it felt like I could hear it.

"Morning." He kissed me and I rolled over and away from him, squeezing the bridge of my nose. I knew I had to get up to feed the pigs and get on with my day, so I felt around the floor for some clothes with my eyes still shut and found my jeans and the old t-shirt I had stolen from him several months before. The window nearest us was open and a breeze blew cool air into the bedroom, which felt nice on my face and helped my overall feeling of exhaustion and lack of motivation. I took a deep breath, then remembered we had company, which meant that instead of nursing my hangover, I'd have to entertain everyone. Hopefully no one else was awake yet. "I'll meet you down there."

I crept downstairs as quietly as I could and found Trey's clogs to slip on my feet while Japhy trailed behind me. "Shhh, buddy," I said, as if that would stop his nails from clicking against the hardwood floor. When I opened the door to the back porch, goosebumps spread over my bare arms. I could hear the few pigs we still had, happily snorting in their pens, and the game birds chirping in theirs. Being outside calmed my nerves and hangover-related uneasiness, so I took my time feeding the animals. But eventually I moseyed back to the house to face everyone. As I approached the back porch, a guitar melody danced out of the open door. I followed the strumming into the kitchen.

"Bree!" Patricio exclaimed when I turned the corner. Patricio was Pedro's brother and a musician, and he'd agreed to play his acoustic guitar during our wedding ceremony. "Happy wedding day, *amiga*!" He continued to strum a pretty folk song I'd never heard before. His wife and daughter had come along for the event and they sat alongside him in our sunny farmhouse kitchen while Trey worked on pancakes.

"I'm thinking of a few songs for tonight, I've been practicing the ones you liked."

"Thanks so much for helping us out man," Trey replied, delivering a heaping plate of hot pancakes to the table.

"I've gotta run—getting ready starts really soon," I said. The clock on the wall ticked away, its hands signaling nearly 11 AM. *This is really happening, I'm getting married*, I thought, *and I'm late.*

I cut my pancake into three equal pieces and shoved them in my mouth in rapid succession, then ran upstairs to grab my makeup bag and bounded back down the steps again.

"Bye!" I yelled as I swirled past the kitchen and hurried to the car.

With my hands full, clicking the button on my car's key fob was basically impossible. "Dammit!" I said to no one in particular. When I eventually succeeded in opening the door I immediately reached for the pack of Parliament Lights that sat on the passenger seat. I lit one before I turned the key in the ignition, took a deep breath, and felt the tension release in my shoulders. In the fog of my nicotine buzz, I started the engine and thought of my parents; I wondered how they would manage the day. I wondered if my mom would hide her tears and if other people would notice that they weren't shed out of happiness. I wondered if my dad would hold his tongue or if the pills he was taking would rid him of his inhibitions. Before I knew it, I was pulling into my parents' driveway.

I sat in the kitchen while people pranced around me, a parade of makeup and hair and tweezing. After the primping was complete, I walked alone upstairs to my childhood room, which looked oddly small since the last time I had been in it. It looked different and felt different although the blue clouds I had painted with a sponge in the seventh grade still populated the high ceiling. The Realtor said that staging was important because new buyers had to imagine themselves in your house, which meant it no longer looked like my home. It was now a blank slate for someone else's memories. My bed sat against the wall that was once full of trophies and medals from my high school swimming days. They had all been placed in boxes along with the rest of my things—my high school scrapbook, my black boom box I got for Christmas in 1995, trinkets and souvenirs, and all the physical objects I had amassed over the course of my life—when the house went up for sale.

My friends filtered upstairs to watch me get dressed and I pulled my wedding dress off its satin hanger. I felt awkward, like I was playing house and not old enough to be getting married. I walked into the dress and slipped the delicate cap sleeves over my shoulders while I twisted toward my mom so she could zipper me up. My friends watched me, and I felt embarrassed by all the attention.

"You look beautiful," my mother said, and I knew she meant it.

When it was time, I held the train of my wedding dress in front of me with both hands so it wouldn't touch the driveway and we piled into my friend Jenny's blue Honda Civic. She popped the cork of a bottle of champagne and passed it to me over the stick shift, so I took a large swig and passed it back to Kristen, who did the same and afterwards stated calmly: "Holy shit, you're getting married."

Our wedding turned out to be beautiful and in the photos that Trey's father took, we looked happy. I felt happy. We said our vows and Trey squeezed my hand as we walked down the trail and away from where all of our family and friends had gathered to watch us. My little brother delivered a speech about organic vegetables that left everyone laughing and we danced to a spanish song by an Argentine singer about a man who had finally found his true love. After a few hours Trey wanted to leave, so we left our wedding before any of our other guests and returned home to the empty farmhouse carrying the delicate petit-fours and cookies we hadn't stayed long enough to eat.

The day after our wedding we drove up to the Catskill Mountains in New York state, and as soon as we arrived we proceeded to order an abundance of drinks in an attempt to slow down the frantic pace we had gotten used to during the farm season. Despite the serenity of the place, neither of us could relax. I didn't tell him how nervous I felt about our upcoming international move. We enjoyed the hiking trails and the couples massage and on our last day away I smoked a joint and settled onto a bench overlooking the mountains to enjoy the scenery. But something felt off. Really, everything felt off. I tried to focus on the late afternoon sun hitting the pine trees and the glassy lake in front of me to calm myself down and preserve my buzz but I couldn't shake a feeling of dread, like the bottom was dropping out of my life. I felt claustrophobic in my own body.

It's okay, it will be okay, I said to myself.

I didn't know what was happening to me, but I desperately wanted it to stop. My focus was like a bouncing ball, erratic and uncontrollable. My palms started to sweat.

Just then Trey yelled from inside the hotel, "Hey, it's time to check out, let's hit it."

"Coming!" I replied and put on my sunglasses. "I'm okay," I said to the vast space in front of me. It was time I got used to feeling uncomfortable.

LANDED

November, 2009

My plane touched down in Santiago de Chile on a sunny day in late November. I had spent the majority of the flight drinking Chilean red wine and flirting with a handsome American expat seated next to me. When I arrived at customs, tired and anxious after the twelve hour flight, I tried to act normal. Acting normal was difficult however, considering the fact that I was carrying ten thousand dollars worth of large bills stuffed in my shoes, carry-on, and pockets. We had split the grand savings we had accumulated over a season of farming—which totaled a little over twenty-thousand dollars—between the two of us. Since Trey had entered the country with his share of the money without issue, I hoped it would be equally easy for me.

I spun my red suitcase around to face me and stepped into a line that had formed while I nervously looked around. *Did they just say they were searching for drugs and fruit?* They were speaking Spanish so quickly I could barely understand. They repeated whatever they had said in English but I couldn't make that out, either. Meanwhile, Labrador Retrievers dressed with olive green vests sniffed at my fellow passenger's luggage. I averted my eyes from the police officers and decided to study the signs that decorated the walls with large Xs around pictures of fruit, cheeses, and cured meats. *Could dogs sniff out dollars?* After ten agonizing minutes, it was my turn.

I loaded my unwieldy luggage onto the belt and stepped through the scanner. The Chilean security guard looked me up and down with a cursory glance and motioned me to continue on my way while both the security dog and its handler had shifted their focus from the line where I stood to another group. *Holy shit, that was it!* I was cleared to go. I tried not to show obvious relief on my face.

I rolled through the clear sliding doors into the pickup area, hurrying, passing groups of people waiting on arrivals. Trey appeared out of nowhere, blonde and tall and ready for me.

"You made it—no issues?"

"Nope, all good."

"Awesome. Shuttle is waiting," he said, as he grabbed my suitcase and led the way out of the airport into the parking lot. A few steps later we emerged from the shade of the airport awning into the sun. The moment the dry heat hit my skin, I felt my body relax. Thank God for summer. We loaded ourselves into the van and began to make our way out of the desert outskirts and into the city. The *cordillera* peaks stared back at me from my window.

Did we really live here now?

We had pre-paid a small fortune on two weeks' rent for a tiny first floor apartment in *Barrio Yungay*, an artsy neighborhood west of the city center, so we would have somewhere to land when we arrived. Our focus, along with figuring out an income stream, was to find a cheaper long-term apartment as quickly as possible before those two weeks were up.

The van stopped abruptly in front of an ornately decorated old building that looked like it had been plucked directly from some European city. The driver directed us to get out. Trey held open one of the heavy wooden doors which led into an open-air terrace with two stories of apartments peering down into it from above. The sounds of metal music played loudly from an open window above my head. There was a faint smell of cigarettes and floral-scented cleaning supplies.

"This one's us," Trey said, pointing to the corner apartment, a big, black, and mostly excited Labrador wagged his tail from just behind its glass doors.

"Good boy, Japh!" I said and knelt down to say hello. "I missed you buddy!" The sight of our old dog in our new Chilean apartment was odd. Japhy also seemed more nervous than usual, which didn't surprise me, since he was the most resistant to change out of the three of us.

Barrio Yungay was a prime location from which to begin our adventure: close to inexpensive subway travel, safe enough, and a rich cultural heritage that made us feel like we were actually in a foreign country. There wasn't a Starbucks or McDonald's in sight and at the time, the neighborhood seemed to be populated by punks, hippies, old alcoholics, and real estate entrepreneurs. There was so much to see and do. We watched a group of dancers from the north of the country perform for the reburial of a prominent Communist folk artist who had been murdered during the dictatorship. We talked with the owner of the building we were renting and he showed us the Andes peaking over the clouds as we discussed how the city was changing. We met up with Pedro and his family and they fed us a cake called *mil hojas* that was layered with their version of caramel.

We settled into a routine, scouring the local newspapers for teaching job listings and apartments downtown, while I gave Trey a crash course in English grammar. A prerequisite to teaching English anywhere is passing an exam to show mastery of the rules and conventions of the language, so one can pass those along to students. We applied to every single language institute that existed in Santiago, and some of them actually invited us in for an interview. Unfortunately, we failed the English exam at both of the major institutes at the top of our list. The day we found out we had failed, we walked together to the corner store to drown our worries in red wine and cigarettes.

"I thought I knew this stuff better than that," Trey said, as he thanked the store clerk and slumped down on the sidewalk, legs propped up on the hot pavement. We peeled the wrapper off the cigarette pack we had just bought and realized we hadn't brought our lighter.

"What if we can't get anything?" I asked, hoping for reassurance.

"It'll be fine, we'll find something."

Our first week in Santiago came to a close, leaving us just seven days to find jobs and an apartment. There was one institute left on our list, but it was far enough uptown that we had saved it for last.

I tugged on jeans and a conservative white blouse the day we walked to the subway for our last interview. We descended the stairs of the Metro, hand in hand, sweating profusely and cursing the fact that neither of us had dressed appropriately for the weather. The subway arrived quickly, I followed him onto the car, and we found a spot near a metal pole to hang onto. It reminded me of New York, but without the tell-tale smell of hot garbage. I looked around at the strangers I now shared my world with. The contrast between me and Trey and the people surrounding us on the subway car was stark. There weren't any other obvious tourists on the car—blonde and tall and speaking English—so I looked at the ground and kept quiet, eyeing the subway map on the wall once in a while to make sure we were headed in the right direction.

Tobalaba, the loudspeaker eventually said—our stop was next.

The train rumbled into the station and the majority of the passengers piled out and rushed off to their jobs while we stared upwards in search of a sign to tell us where to go. We eventually found our exit and hustled up the stairs, carefully avoiding the vendors selling trinkets and leggings at the mouth of the subway station. Tobalaba was a busy hub in the middle of the upper-class commercial area of the city. It was populated with folks rushing to their jobs in finance and mining, most of them in their suits and dressy skirts, hurriedly smoking cigarettes. I yanked a street map out of my bag and flipped it open to the Providencia section of town and found the big red M on the page to mark my spot.

"I think we need to go straight for a little while on Providencia, then turn left on Los Leones," I said. I was generally bad at directions, but these seemed simple enough. Trey agreed, so we started off toward our last hope for finding English teaching jobs before summer hit.

As we walked, I looked around at the men in white jumpsuits who cleaned sidewalks and pedestrian passes with hoses, and the others who watered colorful flowers in beds that lined the fancy residences and businesses. There were bright green, manicured lawns. It looked so different here from downtown. We turned right on Los Leones and saw the sign for the institute about a hundred yards in front of us.

"Oh man there it is, I'm nervous," I said to him.

"You'll be fine."

We walked in, printed resumes in hand, and asked the receptionist if we could speak to the person in charge of hiring. I realized at that moment that we should have emailed to make an appointment first but the sweater-wearing woman excused herself to go find the hiring manager and instructed us to sit down and wait. After about fifteen minutes, a frazzled man shuffled down the stairs wearing a loose tie and khakis.

"Hi guys, I'm Carlos. Nice to meet you. Let's go into a meeting room," he said, motioning toward an empty office behind him.

"I'm Trey, this is my wife Bree," Trey started, after we all sat down and made ourselves comfortable. It was still strange to hear him refer to me as his wife. "We brought our resumes; we're looking for work teaching English. Just arrived last week from the States."

I handed over my resume, smiled and pushed my shoulders back to sit up straight, remembering what my dad had taught me growing up. Around the room were bookshelves lined with English language books, grammar texts, and dictionaries.

"Great, so have you taught English before? How long will you be living here?"

"I taught in Argentina," I lied. "And I have my ESL certificate," I added, which was true.

Trey explained, "I taught English and Spanish language in the States and have a master's degree," omitting the fact that his master's wasn't in English.

"Great, interesting," Carlos said as he scanned our resumes. "You will have to take a test to show your English proficiency and aptitude, but it shouldn't be hard for you both. Would you like to take it now?"

"Sure, yeah let's do that," Trey replied.

"Okay, give me five minutes."

He returned fifteen minutes later with two test packets. "Follow me," he said. Trey was led to a classroom upstairs with windows that overlooked the busy intersection below while I sat in an adjacent room with blue corporate carpeting. I scanned the test and expected the worst, but it was simpler than the others we had taken and we finished quickly, then met outside for a celebratory cigarette.

"I think I aced it," I said between puffs.

"Time will tell."

Thankfully, we didn't need much time. Carlos called the next day to tell us that we had both passed the test. Less than a week later, we were plied with textbooks and starting our first jobs in Chile. There was no time to rest though—we still had an apartment to find.

Trey took the lead on apartment inquiry calls since I could barely understand Chilean Spanish in person, let alone over the phone, but most places had already been scooped up by the time we called or they were quick to turn us down because we were foreigners with no proven income. We would need a Chilean co-signer, we quickly learned, if we were ever going to find a place to live. Thankfully, our Chilean buddy Pedro was happy to help. Three days before our short-term lease was up, an apartment became available in Barrio Lastarria, directly in front of the Cerro Santa Lucía, which was exactly the neighborhood where we had hoped to live. With Pedro's assistance, we scheduled a showing and assured the owner that we had a Chilean co-signer to ease her mind.

The four of us—Trey, Pedro, the owner Claudia, and I—met in front of the entrance to 374 Calle Rosal. There were dozens of newly constructed apartment buildings around downtown but this structure was anything but new. I looked up at the grey cinder block building where floor to ceiling windows overlooked the street and Tibetan prayer flags hung suspended from balconies decorated with ceramic pots overflowing with flowers.

We headed inside and I tried to follow the conversation, but it was so fast and nuanced that I could barely keep up and Claudia corrected my pronunciation when I tried to make small talk.

The antique metal elevator slowly inched its way upwards and arrived at the seventh floor, where we all shuffled out into a skinny hallway with bare, cream-colored walls. Almost immediately Claudia stopped in front of a dark brown door, unlocked it, and we filed directly into the living room of the tiny one-bedroom apartment. The furniture was sparse, all antiques, with two tan velvet armchairs facing one another and a matching love seat on the back wall with a window that looked out onto the Andes mountains and the residential buildings that rose up before them.

I peeked into the kitchen (just big enough to fit one person, either at the sink or the stove) which connected the living room to the bedroom. Since there was only one other area of the apartment to review, the bedroom, we moved there, sharing a few comments about the furniture and the view. Despite the smog, I could see the Andes from this room too.

The apartment would cost double what we wanted to spend but we didn't have the luxury of time, so after a quick conversation about our lack of bank accounts and credit, we persuaded Claudia to let us lease it by putting down six months' rent as a gesture of good faith. A few days and a number of hours in a Chilean notary later, we were the proud new residents of 71 Calle Rosal in Barrio Lastarria, Santiago de Chile.

I had a new husband, a new job, and a new apartment in a foreign country. We had been preparing for over a year in anticipation of this moment and now we were actually doing the thing we had set out to do.

SHAKY
February, 2010

I settled into the velvet love seat underneath the window. There was no air conditioning in the apartment and the fuzzy fabric touching my body didn't help the heat, but I was getting used to the summer in Santiago, hot and hazy with a smog that sat like a blanket between the Andes and the clouds. I lit a cigarette and poured black coffee from the french press, which was my morning routine that followed me no matter where I lived. I stared blankly out the open window while my thoughts turned to the money that sat hidden under the flimsy mattress in the bedroom, our entire savings in US dollars, our future in crisp hundred dollar bills. Lately, I'd walk into the room and find Trey counting them; I'd see the breath catch in his throat, I'd notice him forcing an exhale. "We have to ration this out," he'd say, splaying out a few hundreds to change at the exchange house downtown. "Forty dollars a week if we can, at least until the money starts coming in from teaching." And I'd agree.

When we first arrived we had spent afternoons lounging in internet cafes and drinking *cafe con leche*, but now, with our disposable income shrinking, we stopped going out altogether. And while both the land we would buy and our plans for it existed only in our minds, "the house project" started to become the topic of the majority of our conversations. We had a little less than a year to sort out where we would buy land and start building our off-grid house, since our apartment was only paid for through December. I was used to being a traveler and a tourist, someone who ate out and drank out and spent money I didn't always have. But this time was different—this time I was an expat and we weren't leaving.

Trey joined me for a minute on the couch, asking when I'd be ready to head down to La Vega Central, a sprawling farmers' market close to the bank of the Mapocho River where everyone from the upper-class family's nanny to the downtown chef went to buy their supplies for the week. We visited every weekend, making the slow trek down through the Parque Forestal and across the river, where vendors lined both sides of the street. I'd stop to grab a bag or two of hot sauce made from red habanero peppers that we'd pour over everything from eggs to tacos. Or I'd spend a few pesos on *merkén*, the spice of the Mapuche people who were indigenous to Chile, made from a smoked pepper called the *ají cacho de cabra*.

The vendors there sold everything you could imagine, vibrant fruits and vegetables from the nearby agricultural regions, cuts of meat and live poultry, fresh fish from the Pacific, eggs in open cartons by the dozen, held together by string. It was impossible to visit every vendor, so it was necessary to choose your favorites and stick with them and sometimes they'd remember you if you visited them often enough. I learned new vocabulary for the colorful foods from the yellow signs that stuck out of their bins. And the people who manned the stalls were friendly, always eager to understand us, wanting to know our story and what had brought us to their tiny sliver of a country in the south. Tiny mom-and-pop restaurant stands were scattered in the indoor market, too. They filled their two-top tables with *empanadas,* clear broth soups, and fresh *marraqueta,* the simple and delicious Chilean bread. Folks drank tall beers from reusable green glass bottles and stayed for a while among the feral cats that loped along and slept on the market stands. I looked forward to our time there every week.

Returning home from La Vega one particularly hot Sunday, our arms charged with our weekly ration of groceries, I started to feel strange and agitated, a wave of unease sweeping over me like a flash. The physical sensation made my mind race—*What's happening?* I thought. I forced a few quick steps, just enough to cross a busy pedestrian street beside the Mapocho. Out of the corner of my eye I saw that the water descending into the river from the Andes had dried up.

"Are you okay?" Trey asked, when he noticed. "I don't feel right," I replied, dropping my bags on the steps of a building, trying to catch my breath. I held my head in my sweating palms while time stretched out and the two of us sat in silence on the steps until my heartbeat slowed and I had calmed down enough to go home. *What was that?* A moment before, we had been laughing and taking silly pictures of one another in the market and the next I was in a panic, huddled up on the sidewalk. I thought of myself as a free-living adventurer—how could I be anxious?

The next night over dinner at home we heard a knock on the door. I pushed away my plate and opened the door to find a thirty-something bald man and a blonde woman standing in our doorway.

"Hi there, I'm your neighbor. My name's Daniel. I live right there." The man had a posh British accent and motioned to the apartment diagonal to ours. "Could we possibly use your refrigerator? We're scientists and need to keep this cool but our fridge is broken," he said, holding up a small vial of liquid.

"I'm Camila," the woman chimed in. "We work together, I live here too."

"Yeah of course, any time" I replied, happy to communicate in English with someone other than my husband. Besides our elderly doorman and our students, we hadn't made any friends since our arrival and I was desperate for social interaction.

"Great, nice meeting you. We'll come back tomorrow for it. Thanks very much," Daniel said.

"Maybe we could hang out with them sometime?" I asked Trey after they had left.

"Yeah maybe," Trey replied, but it was clear his focus was on our project, not making friends.

That night before bed, we walked the dog through Parque Forestal, a verdant stretch that occupied a good portion of downtown Santiago. The night was warm and breezy and we took our time. Later, we shared a bottle of cheap red wine while we read books we had already read and smoked the last of a pack of Lucky Strike cigarettes.

At 3:30AM we woke to Japhy whining at the foot of our bed. He never woke us up.

"Go to bed, buddy," Trey said.

I rolled over and shut my eyes. But Japhy cried louder, trying to communicate something we weren't understanding. He walked over to Trey's side of the bed and the shaking started. At first, it was only a slight tremble. We had experienced a few tremors since arriving, so thought nothing of it—Chile is known for being a seismic country after all—but then the movement grew and the bedroom began to sway violently from side to side.

I screamed for Trey while we scrambled out of bed, him grabbing Japhy by the collar and then putting his hand out to lead me into the bathroom where we pressed our backs against the tiled bathroom wall as the earthquake shook off our sleep.

This is no ordinary earthquake, I thought, as I looked around and realized what was happening. The force that shook our building was so strong I wondered if the building would break in two. And then I thought about my parents, and what would happen if I died here in the rubble of a natural disaster. I looked up—we were still crouching together on the bathroom floor—to see the mirrors that hung on opposite sides of the bathroom wall jumping from their usual locations to meet one another in the middle of the air above our heads. Everything crumbled and jumped around us. Glassware crashed to the ground and frames fell from the walls. In every room there were people just like us, praying for the shaking to end.

Shouldn't it have stopped by now?

Then the lights flickered out around the city and there was eerie, total darkness all around while our building continued to sway. I tucked my head between my knees and an interesting thought came to mind: I have no control. No matter what I did, the world would have its way with me—with all of us. I had never considered that even the ground under my feet could suddenly become unstable.

"Oh my god, oh my god," I heard myself saying. Trey wrapped his arms around me and the dog as we continued to shake on the bathroom floor. And then it stopped.

It was just over three minutes even though it seemed like hours. Since we had never been in an earthquake before, we had no idea what to do. Would there be aftershocks? Did we need to leave the building? What did the rest of the city look like? I found our cell phone that had been left in the living room, but there was no signal. We remembered the solar-powered lantern we had stored in the closet and switched it on and I had never been so thankful for a purchase from an outdoor supply company in all my life.

"I want to check in with someone—what about Daniel and Camila, the neighbors?" I asked. I looked down at my shaking hands as I opened the door to the apartment, grateful the door hadn't been jammed shut. Trey and Japhy followed.

"Hello? Hola?" I said in the direction of their apartment. I noticed their door was open but knocked anyway.

"Hello, yes?" Daniel replied.

"Hey, it's Bree and Trey, your neighbors," Trey said. "Just wanted to check in, you guys okay?"

"Yeah yeah, come on in," Daniel answered from inside.

It was a strange circumstance for a first-time invitation and I could see their place was much larger than ours. Cigarette smoke floated inside from the balcony, where the two roommates stood.

"Holy fuck can you believe that?" Daniel asked.

"No man, holy shit. That was insane." Trey replied in solidarity.

"I've lived here for months and there've been some tiny tremors, but nothing like that," Daniel continued. "Look at the road," he added, offering Trey a cigarette.

I walked over to the metal railing of the balcony to peer down at the pavement and saw that the road had rippled, like a wave.

"My god this is crazy," I said. "Our building seems to be okay though."

Camila replied: "They're built to withstand earthquakes here, especially these old, solid ones. New construction, not so much."

"Beer, anyone?" Daniel asked to lighten the mood.

We accepted the cold beer and spent the rest of the early

morning in an adrenaline-fueled conversation about Chile and about life, who we were and why we had come and what we were planning to do.

The earthquake, we later found out, had been one of the largest and longest in the country's history, measuring an 8.8 on the Richter scale at its center. It was the strongest to hit Chile since 1960. The shifting of the tectonic plates in the Pacific subsequently caused a tsunami that threw waves as high as fifty feet down the southern coast, laying waste to ports in Concepción and Talcahuano. The majority of buildings had been built to stringent earthquake guidelines after the 9.5 quake that had occurred decades earlier, but many older buildings in the south and elsewhere sustained serious damage. Our sturdy building had survived unscathed, save a few superficial cracks in the plaster walls. We were lucky. A NASA computer model found that the force had shifted the Earth's axis enough to shorten the day on earth by more than a microsecond.

Afterward, the country began the lengthy process of reconstruction and for weeks the earthquake was the only topic of conversation on everyone's lips. As with any tragedy, we traded stories about where we were when it happened, how it felt and what, if anything, we had lost. I gained a vocabulary for explaining terror, aftershocks, and gratitude. And for the first time since arriving, we had a shared experience with the Chilean people.

STEPS

May, 2010

We would construct an off-grid house without a mortgage. Without a large financial obligation every month, we would be freed of ties to conventional jobs. We would rely on the land, and our ingenuity, to build a life that made sustainable sense to us and the natural world around us. We would spend our precious days in all the ways we wanted and rid ourselves of the burden of consumerism and the US and start new. Or at least that was the plan. The plan had materialized in the early drunken days on Trey's parent's back porch on the farm and during our conversations in the basement the following summer. It sounded ambitious every time we spoke it out loud, and our pursuit of it felt like something that separated us from everyone else. It was finally time to put our plan into action. We had been in Chile for six months, it was winter, and our new home felt less foreign than before.

Every moment we weren't working or commuting to work, we spent searching online for a piece of property we could afford. We sat in our bedroom, me with my elbows on my knees, him in charge of the searching on my old Sony computer that would only turn on if it was plugged in perfectly.

We were familiar with Valparaiso, the region northwest of Santiago, and it was close enough to the city that we would be able to make day and weekend trips to work on house construction while still making money teaching classes during the week. Valparaiso itself wasn't rural enough, but smaller neighborhoods outside the city limits were within our budget and some of them were coastal towns with views of the Pacific. I imagined us traipsing around a sleepy little beach town, speaking perfect Spanish to the locals, surfing on the weekends.

After a couple months of fruitless searching—nearly everything we looked into was an old or already sold listing—one potential property caught our eye: a six hundred square meter plot twenty minutes outside of Valparaiso, in a town called Laguna Verde. So we emailed the owner, a man named Adrien, to arrange a visit. We told him we would call when we arrived in Valparaiso and later that week, we hopped on a bus headed towards the coast.

We arrived at the Valparaiso bus terminal and dialed his number. *"Alo?"* Adrien answered, but he didn't sound Chilean. He suggested we meet at his apartment, which was within walking distance from the bus station. Ten minutes later, we were standing outside of his building, looking up at its colorful, aging exterior; it looked like it was once painted mint green but was now a faded shade of sea foam.

I rang the antique bell outside the doorway and heard heavy footsteps descending the stairs to meet us. The door opened and Adrien appeared, tall, broad and French. He was handsome in a soft, friendly way.

"Mucho gusto," Adrien said, *"entra, entra."* His Spanish was near perfect; he later told us he'd been living in Chile for years, but he couldn't rid himself of the obvious French accent.

"Gracias," Trey and I replied in unison.

We followed him upstairs to the open communal living space. There appeared to be several people living there, all of them young. A woman in brightly colored linen pants and a see-through crochet top greeted us with an English "Hello." I felt almost puritanical in my ratty old sweater and jeans.

"This is my girlfriend, Violeta," Adrien added, pointing to another woman who was chopping onions and tomatoes in the canary yellow kitchen. We sat down at the table and conversed in Spanish, as neither he nor Violeta spoke English, and neither Trey nor I spoke French.

"Okay," Adrien began. "So the land is in a residential sector, close to the beach, with lots of native pine trees. It's really beautiful there, lots of good people. I bought an entire hectare and now I'm selling off the pieces. This one has a really nice flat part, perfect for building a house."

He passed us a black and white map with a section marked off with a large X. *Parcelación 1348, Curaumilla, Laguna Verde, Valparaiso.*

"You want to go see it?"

"*Si,* let's go."

Adrien packed the requisite *marraqueta* and hard cheese into plastic bags and suggested we make a quick stop at the shop on the corner for supplies. Once there, we bought a pack of cigarettes and Escudo, the unofficial beer of Chile. I shoved them both into my North Face backpack and Adrien, Violeta, Trey, and I set off toward the bus stop.

A multitude of *micros,* the local transport buses, passed while we stood on the corner. They whizzed by in different color combinations: green and orange, white and green, shades of blue. Adrien said to watch for an orange and green one with *Laguna Verde* written in big black letters on the front windshield, number 520. But the buses hurried into the stop on the corner so quickly, I could barely read the number on the front let alone the words spread out across the windshield.

"Buses come once every twenty minutes or so," Adrien said. "If one just passed, we'll have to wait."

I collected the fare, 550 pesos each or the equivalent of one US dollar, from the change purse of the wallet my parents had bought me in college. Its leather was worn now, but it hinted at a past life full of well-made belongings. The feeling bounced around in my head while I counted the silver and gold-colored pieces in my hand.

Charcoal grill smoke and the aroma of cooking meat wafted toward us from *anticucho* vendors who were stationed around the square. They turned the skewers, dripping with grease, and called out their offerings: "*Anticuchos, empanadas!*" I watched them wrap the fried pockets of dough in flimsy paper napkins, then turned my attention back to the buses. Bus after bus continued to pass, each with another unknown destination displayed on its windshield. Then out of the corner of my eye, I read: **Laguna Verde** in bold black lettering across the front of an orange and green bus that was making its way toward our stop.

"There it is!" I said and all four of us waved the driver down, in case he wasn't planning to stop.

We boarded and made our way to a couple open seats in the back, at which point I noticed a few of our fellow bus riders staring in our direction.

"Laguna isn't popular with tourists—yet," Adrien said in passing, as he and Violeta sat down, positioning themselves directly in front of me and Trey. As the bus meandered through the streets, they kissed and spoke in whispers to one another. I watched them. They were clearly in the throes of new love and seeing them so infatuated with one another made me jealous. Trey and I were newlyweds, shouldn't we be acting like it? We were rarely intimate any longer, and any time I questioned it, or asked for affection he would call me needy and cite how busy we were. I plopped down in my seat, feeling more than a little bad for myself while Trey stared out the window, completely oblivious to my inner turmoil.

Our little bus jetted through pockets of Valparaiso I hadn't seen before. There was still so much about the city we didn't know. Residential and commercial buildings co-mingled, juxtaposing gray cinder block with intricate European architecture. I looked up from the street to take in the curved balconies and decorative cornices that invoked the opulence of the past. Graffiti decorated the facades of most buildings and I wondered if they had tried to remove it but eventually gave up. Vintage trolleys that we later learned were built in the early 1950s ran parallel to our bus as we approached Plaza Sotomayor, a square flanked by government buildings with a large monument of a soldier in its center. Crowds of tourists congregated around the square in buzzing groups.

We zoomed past them and continued on our journey north, turning abruptly onto a road that ran parallel to the port. One of the famous *funiculares*, antique railways that were built in the 19th century to travel up and down the hills, crept lazily along the mountainside. Then multicolored shipping containers came into view and light blue buildings belonging to the navy. If we decided to move to Laguna, this city would be our home too. We made a sharp turn to the left, started up a hill, and the view began to change.

Adrien twisted himself in his seat, his arm still draped across Violeta's shoulders, and spoke: "Now we're in Playa Ancha."

Short palm trees burst out of the dry ground to the side of the paved road, which led us past an elementary school and a university whose dusty soccer fields were empty. Overgrown bushes poked through chain link fences and cigarette packs and plastic soda bottles littered both sides of the street. As we traveled upwards, stores became fewer and farther between. Pastel-colored homes lived behind gates with metal prongs to keep out intruders. Children's school uniforms were hung out to dry. Venturing further into the hills, the scent of eucalyptus filled the air while feral dogs roamed, skinny and searching. Through the open windows I smelled burning, so I turned around in my seat to locate the fire and instead found the bright blue line of the sea, ever present, reminding me why we had come all this way. Then the road opened up and we passed over a highway and a sign with an arrow pointing straight ahead indicated Laguna Verde.

The majority of passengers had gotten off by then and four ocean-facing window seats were open, so at Adrien's suggestion we slid over to take in what he said would soon be an incredible view. As we finally neared Laguna, the landscape around us changed completely, as if suddenly washed with a deep green from a heavy-handed painter's palette. Eucalyptus trees, tall and straight, popped up on both sides of the road. There were no businesses or homes to speak of. Then suddenly, the thick army of trees disappeared and opened up into a flat plane, where a gang of dogs lay sunbathing. I couldn't see the ocean yet, but by the way Adrien and Violeta stared in anticipation out the window, I knew it had to be close.

Just then, the road up ahead turned so sharply left that it looked like we would fall straight down into nothing—I held my breath. And instantly there it was, the Pacific, dark blue and deep. Mist hung over the hills surrounding Laguna's cove like it was protecting something hidden. And maybe it was—there were only a handful passengers left on the bus. Laguna was still a secret yet to be discovered.

"Oh my god, Trey," I said, watching the ocean breathe in and out below us.

Adrien was right, it was incredible.

As we continued to descend, twisting and turning, the expanse of the coast came into view. Lonely trees grew in pockets along the steep cliff and I tried not to look down at the turbulent white and aqua waves. When we reached the halfway point, the small town at the bottom revealed itself. My eyes lingered on flowers that adorned memorials to those who had perished on the obviously dangerous road.

A few minutes later, we reached the bottom and raced into town, the bus driver waving *hello* to every person who walked by. Small, metal-roofed homes with vibrant flowers and overflowing gardens were spread out through the unmarked streets.

Adrien, who now sat behind us, tapped Trey on the shoulder and said we'd pass through town and be at the property in about fifteen minutes. As we entered the town proper, the road turned from pavement to dusty gravel and we slowed to accommodate the bumps. Then we stopped in front of a small corner store and the driver threw back the e-brake and trod down the stairs.

"Where the hell is he going?" I whispered to Trey. He just shrugged. I looked around, but no one else seemed bothered by the driver's absence.

After a few minutes, when the driver lumbered back onto the bus, he casually sat back down, opened a 10-pack of cigarettes, lit one, and continued to drive. I tried to remember that I was, in fact, not in a hurry.

When our voyage through town was complete, only the four of us remained on the bus and I wondered if the drive would ever end while the bus continued on, now climbing a hill of green. I looked at our changing surroundings. Now that we were out of town, homes of different sizes peppered the hillside, many of them still in various stages of construction. All of them had solar panels and some kind of water-holding receptacle attached to the house. There were no public amenities here, it seemed. We passed a small store whose entire structure was made of skinny eucalyptus trees framed by two Chilean flags. A sign out front advertised the sale of fresh eggs and canisters of natural gas. Pine trees grew tall along the road.

Adrien rose from his seat and walked to the front of the bus. I could hear him telling the driver to let us off at the curve up ahead.

"We get off here, guys," Violeta said, as she motioned for us to make our way to the front.

"We have to walk a little—fifteen, twenty minutes—should we open the beer?"

So I swung my backpack around to the front of me, unzipped it and grabbed the beer. I took a heavy swig and passed it around to Trey, who passed it to Adrien, and to Violeta last.

Adrien started walking in what I assumed was the direction of the house and the rest of us followed. As we ventured further into the woods and away from the main road, the path underneath our feet changed from loose dirt to clay and soon after, the terrain became more difficult to manage. Thank god I wore sneakers, I thought to myself. I tried to take in my surroundings while minding my step, looking around every now and again to take in the changing view as our steps brought us further into the wilderness. Eventually, we were trudging up a dusty red hill, Trey and I blindly following Adrien and Violeta, sneaking glances at one another as if to say, *Well, this sure is off-grid.* The cloud cover overhead had dispersed and was replaced by a bright blue sky. I sucked in the crisp beach air, feeling far from the city.

"*Hola,* Blackie!" Adrien announced when we arrived at an opening in the trees where a single wooden house stood. There had only been a couple other small wooden-paneled shacks on the walk but they looked uninhabited. A black mutt made its way over to us, wagging its tail. "This is Rosa and Ricardo's house," said Adrien. "They're friends of mine, or rather, more like grandparents—*abuelos*. They live in Santiago, but they spend weekends here in the countryside. They're not here now but you'll meet them eventually."

We continued on the trail until we arrived at Adrien's property which housed only a small dwelling that was built on pillars like stilts and from the outside looked to be under construction. He explained that he had cleared the property himself, as no one had ever lived on the piece of land before he bought it. He had torn the prefabricated home down from another location in town and rebuilt it on his plot. Like every house there, it was built on pillars to raise it above the ground so no foundation was necessary.

We made our way up the wooden steps he had built and into the main living quarters, an approximately ten by ten foot space that also encompassed the kitchen, with a floor and walls made of particle board. A white sheet covered the doorway to what I assumed was the bedroom. We had finished the beer we brought, so Adrien opened up a bottle of red wine he had stored in the pantry and asked us if we'd like to go out to the porch to see the view. I couldn't wait to sit down.

We gathered four chairs to face the Pacific and Trey and I looked around. Adrien's property and the adjacent properties he owned sat in the middle of a valley full of pine and other native trees, completely untouched by human hands. His yard was barren and dry like the desert, in stark contrast to the greenery surrounding us on the hills. It seemed that only specific, rugged things thrived there. I'd heard songs about big country, but never experienced somewhere so vast. Green pines stretched as far as I could see, meeting the faint line of the Pacific Ocean on the horizon. The ocean was less than a mile away as the crow flew, though Adrien said walking there would take over an hour. We looked north to the property that could be ours, which was completely covered with young pine trees, save a small clearing in the middle. The ocean breeze hit my cold cheeks and I threw my alpaca scarf over my head to stop the wind, then lit a cigarette after a few tries with a match.

We spent the rest of the afternoon drinking cheap red wine out of shared glasses and discussing the possibilities of building a home and a community in that uninhabited place. We'd improve the soil and grow a garden to share, Adrien said. We all wanted chickens and honeybees someday. Violeta seemed supportive, nodding in silent agreement. I tried to stay engaged with our conversation but wished we'd brought more to drink, like back on the farm, when it seemed we never ran out. I could see Trey's wheels turning as he sketched out house plans in his head.

Smelling of sweat and fresh air, we eventually boarded the bus back to Santiago.

"I liked it, did you?"

"It's beautiful, and we can make it work."

I shifted my tired body in the bus seat to face him. We decided together that if we wanted to build a new life, neither of us could think of an option that fit better than the one right in front of us. It was the beginning. We would buy the land in Laguna. The momentum of our work had led us this far, and it was time to see where the journey took us next.

The following week we met Adrien in Valparaiso to purchase the property, which was an all day ordeal, considering the bureaucratic nightmare that is purchasing assets in Chile. But at the end of the day, we were the proud legal owners of six hundred square meters of coastal ground in Curaumilla, Laguna Verde. The land cost 3,500,000 Chileano Pesos, or the equivalent of seven thousand US dollars.

Since Trey would be doing most, if not all, of the construction himself, we needed to buy a vehicle. And due to our dwindling savings, we had to find something inexpensive that was also durable enough to transport building materials to our off-road property. We figured we could find an affordable option on the internet, not realizing that given the geographical distance from manufacturers, cars, like most consumer goods in Chile, were about double the cost of those in the US.

As the weeks went on, we realized we didn't have the luxury of time. Our year-long lease would be up in a mere six months, at which point we would have to be able to move out to Laguna. We had a little over six months to build something habitable. In a rush and with lowered standards, Trey found a truck on a Chilean classifieds website and, after a brief meeting with its owner, he decided to buy it—a 1983 Nissan Patrol for 1,750,000 Chilean pesos, around three thousand six hundred US dollars. *What a steal*, we thought.

He decided to pick up the new ride alone. I read in the living room while I waited for him to return with our second major purchase—one that would give us the gift of mobility and allow the house project to really begin. I turned the page of my book and took a sip of coffee when I heard a faint, high-pitched noise that I couldn't place. I put my book down to focus on the sound as it got louder and louder. The sound became fuller, with an added layer of noise that mimicked the grinding of gears or a garbage truck with no muffler. The metallic *eeeeeh* sound was so loud that eventually I assumed whatever was making it had to be directly outside my window so I headed downstairs.

As I passed through the doors of our building and onto the busy street, there was Trey, turning the key in the ignition to a beat up red jeep with a removable canvas top and plastic windows, while passers-by gaped at the tall blonde man behind the wheel.

"Holy shit, is this it?" I asked.

"Yup, she's a beast huh?" He threw me the key with a proud look on his face.

We were officially armed with jobs, a piece of land, and a mighty old Beast to build our place and we had done it all within six months of landing in Chile. It wasn't time to celebrate yet, though: our savings had just run out.

SWEAT & DIRT

June, 2010

"I don't feel good," I said and cranked the manual window down to let in the ocean air. It was our first official trip to Laguna as property owners and I was hungover. We'd indulged in too much wine the night before and as usual, my hangover anxiety and guilt was kicking in. Unable to hear the music over the screaming siren of the Beast's engine, I looked out my passenger side window.

The route from Santiago to Valparaiso was a familiar highway, similar to those at home only without the 18-wheelers. In their place limped half-size trucks who coughed fumes into the sky. Directional signs were few and far between and we knew from experience that if you missed your exit, it would take twice the amount of time to double back and figure out where you went wrong. It's not like we had GPS. We kept our eyes peeled for La Polvora, a twisting roller coaster of a road that led to Laguna Verde and nearby Playa Ancha. I spotted the exit a moment before we missed it, and we slowed to a snail's pace around the curved off-ramp.

As we ventured further on La Polvora, Trey kept his eyes on the road ahead, trying to anticipate the curves through the early morning fog that had started to surround us. A horse-drawn cart slowly made its way up the shoulder of the road and a small sedan with two differently-painted doors sputtered next to us. The Beast fit right in.

"Adrien said we're only on this road for about fifteen kilometers, so just hang on, we'll be there soon," Trey said.

"Okay, this road is crazy," I added.

"Yeah no kidding, I'm the one trying to drive on it."

I glanced in the backseat, where Japhy looked about as uneasy as I felt. A cheap blue tent we had purchased from a home improvement store in downtown Santiago was tucked alongside the dog, a brand new yellow cooler, and two large jugs of water. The cooler, filled with cheap sausages, a hunk of cheese, and a baguette shifted in the backseat with every turn.

As we continued, I read the directions Adrien had written out for us on a piece of notebook paper. "Okay, get off here at the exit that says Zeal, then make a left. This is the way we came last time."

"Okay, yeah this looks familiar," Trey replied, and we started on the road that would bring us down the coast. I wiped my sweating hands on my jeans, which were getting tight. I'd have to do something about that, I thought.

As we rounded the corner, the ocean came into view, fog hanging low like clouds over the entire cove. I hung on tightly to the overhead handle and felt nausea rush over me but reminded myself we would be on flat ground soon.

"We keep going on this road, past the curve we got off last time, and then continue straight," I directed as we passed through town. "The directions get a little weird after that," I added.

"What do they say?"

"Well, we make a left at the little yellow house on the left, then it says to go straight until there's a cross in the road."

"Alright, well here's the yellow house," he said as we approached it. "Simple enough." The road had turned into a narrow, red dirt path.

"Now I think we just continue straight until we see a cross in the road, or a place to turn left," I interpreted the Spanish instructions and crude map Adrien had drawn the best I could.

"Is this it?" Trey asked as we turned left into a rocky bank.

"Eh—maybe? No clue," I returned. When the path we chose turned into a dead end, we doubled back.

"Let me see," Trey asked, studying the piece of paper in my hands. "These directions don't make sense, unless we missed it."

After fifteen minutes of circling and searching, we turned left far earlier than we had the first time, and ended up on a road that ran parallel to the one we had been on. The dirt paths were wide enough for two horses to pass one another, but not two cars. I hoped we were the only ones getting lost that day.

"This seems wrong," I said after we had bumped along the path for another few minutes. "Are we sure we're going the right way?"

"I don't know Bree, but that's not helpful." There were no street names or markers, just a few abandoned shacks in a dense pine forest. Even if we saw someone who could help, our destination didn't even have a name. After a few more minutes we came to the conclusion that the directions were useless. We'd have to find a way on our own. Other than the raging motor of the Beast, it was eerily quiet. With the fog and no sunshine to light our way, the strange paths that led into the forest felt ominous. My heartbeat quickened. My hangover wasn't helping.

We doubled back and forged ahead then turned around and were on the brink of losing our minds when finally, after a full hour of searching, we bounced down a small hill and into a clearing where the trees parted. We recognized Rosa and Ricardo's house at the far end.

"Honey, that's it! That's where we need to go—this is right!" I shouted.

"Holy shit, finally."

Once we reached the end of the man-made path in front of Adrien's house, Trey turned off the engine and we got out to stretch our legs. Hoping water would help my fragile state, I chugged feverishly from the plastic jug and took a look around. The air was much cooler than in Santiago. I tugged my white wool hat down to cover my long greasy hair.

"We're going to have to make our own path, since this one stops here. It's about a hundred yards until we reach our property line," Trey said, stomping out a cigarette in the wet dirt and grass. "I've got a hatchet and a branch saw, those will have to do."

"Alright, so, you want us to clear all of these trees and branches from here until there?" I asked, sweeping my hand across an imaginary line in the air. I didn't know how I would summon the energy to do physical labor. I looked up to see Trey already hacking away on the larger trees and tearing them out by the roots, a man on a mission.

I took a deep breath and started working on pines with skinny trunks, snapping branches, twisting and turning and yanking each one out of the soil with my new yellow gloves. I knelt and worked and when my legs went numb I sat, shifting and changing position to get a better grip. The wet soil smelled like spring even though it wasn't. I'd take a break from pulling trees to clear up sticks and branches that were strewn across the grass, making piles to be burned later for fire. My hands and knees hurt but eventually my hangover was replaced by a dull, tired ache. After a few focused hours, we turned around to see that we had forged the path, creating something obviously ours through the middle of the pine trees.

When it was time to set up camp for the night, we chose a flat, cleared piece of the land that would eventually become the footprint for our house. Trey showed me how to set up the tent (it was my first time camping). Next, he started building a fire for us to cook our dinner. I watched intently as he chose wood from the piles we had created, placing larger logs down and layering smaller branches and sticks on top to form a pyramid, then lighting it with careful and patient skill. I cut copious slices of the block of hard cheese we had brought and made sandwiches with the chewy bread, shoving them in my mouth as fast as I could. Trey continued to clear trees as I ate ravenously. Normally, I'd feel ashamed for eating that way, but normal didn't apply anymore. Then, we threw fatty sausages on a frying pan we had brought and I watched them crackle on the makeshift stovetop over the fire. After we had eaten, I sat back, satisfied with our meal, and lifted my gaze to take in the view.

The valley where we sat was now covered in shadows, but the setting sun cast light on the hills that made them look like they were glowing. I looked over at Trey as he finished his meal. He always looked like he was planning something, remembering something, onto the next thing, even while he was sitting still. And although the scenery around us was peaceful, my insides were jumping as

I realized that the project was finally happening and I was actually going to live off-the-grid in Chile. *What have I gotten myself into?* I wanted to retreat into something familiar and then had a terrifying feeling it was no longer possible. I did everything I could to stave off a panic attack until eventually the fire went out and we made our bed of old blankets with the dog curled up beside us. I inched in closer to both of them to keep warm, and finally fell asleep, too exhausted to let any more thoughts materialize in my brain.

We woke up after our first night on the property, cold, in our clothes from the day before, smelling of campfire and stale cigarettes. The only sound was the chirping of birds. I realized there was no one around us, maybe for miles. I gazed awhile at the greenery surrounding us, a mix of some kind of pine tree with rounded branches that reached toward the sky and a woody plant with odd-looking red flowers. My back was stiff from sleeping on the hard ground but the little sleep I had gotten had calmed my rattled brain. *I can handle this*, I thought, as I gathered sticks to make a fire for coffee.

If I could re-frame the project as a challenge, a test to be overcome, I knew I could push through. I was sure the hard work would be worth it in the end. By the time I had finished my first cup of coffee, Trey had already started on the day's work of clearing the footprint for the house and I realized I had better start helping. His determination was palpable. He moved with an urgency that started to rub off on me; I tried to work hard, wanting to please him, but by lunchtime I was itching to take a break and told him so. I knew he would have rather spent the entire day working, but in an effort to make me happy, he agreed to spend the rest of the day exploring the coastline. We remembered Adrien telling us about a hidden beach called Las Docas, a place so secluded and remote, only local Chileans knew about it.

We packed up the dog, beer, and our digital camera in the Beast and made off toward the secret beach. We knew the general direction of the cove, due west of our property, so we pounded down the dirt roads in search of the right route. At our first fork in the road we found a sign marked *Playa*, from there following a worn-down dirt path until, about twenty minutes later, we arrived at a cleared outlook and a trail that led straight down to the beach.

I hopped out of the car. Looking down I saw a jagged shoreline and sharp rock formations peering out from clear turquoise water. The cove of Las Docas was unlike any beach I had ever seen. In order to access the beach, we had to carefully scale a narrow, almost vertical trail carved into rock. We walked around to see if there was an alternative way down but couldn't find one so we inched our way with cautious feet, Japhy sandwiched between us, the most cautious of all. Once all three of us had touched down on the sand, we looked around and realized we were all alone. A small shack sat in the middle of the coastline, its purpose unclear. The sea in front of us whipped the shore with waves, crashing, wild and untamed. Even though I was an avid swimmer, I cuffed my jeans, dipped my toes in the icy water, and backed off toward safety. I wasn't going to risk being swept away. Trey, on the other hand, ripped his clothes off and happily jumped in while I watched, laughing nervously from the windy shore. After a bit of swimming he dried off and we spent an hour drinking beer and exploring the dank empty caves hidden within the rock formations that hugged the cove. *This secret beach is a gift*, I thought later, as we shook the sand from our bare feet and headed back to our property. I promised myself I'd do my best to enjoy it.

We returned to Laguna the following two weekends to continue clearing the property and break ground. We were learning that projects always took longer to complete than we anticipated, but we were settling into a rhythm and we had our routine. As soon as we arrived to the land each weekend we'd quickly get to work setting up. I'd lay the blue tarp on the flattest piece of ground that sat directly in front of the soon-to-be house and start pitching the tent, spreading out blankets and pillows from our apartment to cozy up our sleeping arrangement. He'd unload supplies, as much as he had been able to fit in the Beast, and get to work immediately. I sat on the ground with Japhy by my side and watched Trey create the footprint of the house with blue string hung between sticks, one for each corner, a tiny square where our house would eventually stand. Then, he dug hollow PVC piping into the ground where each pillar would support the house, using a two by four, a level, and string, tied and pulled from pillar to pillar, in an attempt to level set each one on the slanted land.

At the end of June, we traveled to Laguna with the goal of pouring the cement pillars that the house would sit on. Neither of us had any experience pouring cement so we relied on the internet and a house-building book Trey had brought with him from the States; we mixed the cement powder with water from jugs we had bought in town, then shook the mixture on a tarp to achieve the right consistency. Once it was ready, we slowly poured the sludge into the open PVC to create each pillar, twenty in total, which would create a sturdy foundation for the house. It was messy, tedious work. When the pillars were poured, Trey set metal brackets in each one to hold the two-by-fours that would create the base of the house.

Weeks passed this way until the following month he was able to add two layers of flooring. Once laid, it was far from perfect—but a slanted floor made of plywood beat sleeping on the hard ground any day. And winter was coming, which meant that even if we weren't sure how to do it, the roof had to be completed before the rains came to the coast. If we weren't able to construct the roof, the newly-set floors would be ruined.

Back in Santiago, we were struggling to make ends meet. Having exhausted our savings on the land, truck, building supplies, and a year of rent, we were forced to rely on our small income from English teaching to sustain ourselves. While our English classes were consistent, there just weren't enough of them. Most weekends we traveled to Laguna to work on the house, but occasionally we'd lack the funds for gas or supplies, so we'd spend the weekend eating boxed mac and cheese in front of the tiny television in our bedroom, planning the next piece of the house-building puzzle.

On an unusually lazy Sunday, we were invited to dinner at our friend Jen's place in Ñuñoa, a middle-class residential area in the northeastern part of the city. Jen was a petite, fun-loving woman from Wisconsin who was the manager of the teacher's training program where we worked. We had exchanged numbers after the class was finished in an attempt to make new friends and I was thrilled when she called. We took a bus to the apartment she shared with her husband; after arriving, the doorman buzzed us upstairs. We walked into their apartment, Stevie Wonder's *Greatest Hits* playing softly over the speaker, and saw Jen and her husband Juan frying up homemade *empanadas* in their galley-style kitchen. The smell of vegetable oil filled the apartment.

I reached out to shake Juan's hand but quickly remembered how awkward a handshake could be in a cheek-kissing country. "*Mucho gusto,*" I said.

"Nice to meet you guys," he replied in perfect English.

"So glad you two are here. Come on in, make yourselves comfortable. Red wine?" Jen popped the cork of the Chilean Cabernet.

"It's our favorite." Trey helped himself to a glass and started toward the living room.

"You guys smoke, right?" Juan asked. He had silently gone to a bedroom and brought back a box he now opened. The skunky smell of good weed drifted toward us.

We made our way to the couch and eventually, Juan asked what had brought us to Chile. We were always excited to share our homesteading dream, so Trey happily obliged.

"Well, we came here with some money to buy land in the countryside," Trey began. "I want to build a house there and be completely self-sustaining. We found a little piece of land in the Quinta Region, around Valparaiso. I'm looking into solar panels, maybe wind power too, depending." He was so self-assured, even though we had barely started the project. His confidence was contagious. Juan and Jen seemed impressed with our plans and continued to ask questions. "We'd love to do that someday," they admitted, as we made our way to the dining room table for dinner.

We were busy shoveling empanadas into our mouths when a brief knock on the door was followed by a young woman with long blonde hair walking in. She explained that she had come to pick up a dime bag of weed from our hosts.

"This is Sam," Jen said. "She's lived here a while too."

"I'm originally from Wisconsin. Are you English teachers?" Sam asked, pouring herself a glass of red wine. Apparently she had decided to join us.

"Yup, and we like it, but they're just not giving us enough classes," I answered.

"Well, I'm a coordinator for an English institute, actually. We're always looking for good teachers. Shoot me an email and I'll make an intro to the team in charge of hiring," she said.

"Wow, that would be amazing, thanks," I replied, and quickly jotted down her email address. Our host passed a perfectly rolled joint in her direction and she quickly took a puff and waved goodbye.

After dinner the men got up to discuss books or music or look at Juan's weed paraphernalia, leaving Jen and me to ourselves on the patio. She passed me the joint. I hadn't smoked since we left the States, and I took a lengthy drag. Instantly, I felt the familiar cloudy buzz of marijuana, a friend I hadn't visited in months. The high was a body memory of countless hangouts, parties, solitary scenes, happiness. And now I was in Chile, disconnected from the familiar footing of home. But instead of panicking, I relaxed into the moment, took a second drag, and another feeling shimmied its way into my consciousness. The thought came from somewhere deep inside me, as high musings sometimes do. I felt an overwhelming understanding that this life was meant to be an adventure and that we were on the precipice of something big. I looked out into the Santiago night, at the lights illuminating the darkened streets of Ñuñoa, and felt proud.

FANCY, SHINY THINGS
July, 2010

I eventually wrote to Sam and arranged an interview at the uptown office of the institute where she worked. Trey and I both knew that if we really wanted to make our house project happen, we'd have to start pulling in much larger paychecks. A new job or two could be the ticket out of our hand-to-mouth existence.

The rain started early on the day of my interview at Smart English. I peeked through our bedroom window, but the dreary view was unsurprising. Winter in Santiago meant rain. And not just any rain, but an unforgiving cold that seeped into your core and made warming up nearly impossible, especially since Trey and I only had a couple sweaters and one winter jacket between the two of us.

After a quick subway ride uptown I sloshed into the office, soggy, with drenched hair, wearing Trey's old winter coat and a ratty sweater I had found in a consignment shop back home. I was ashamed at what I saw when I accidentally caught my reflection in the mirrored walls of the elevator. I had put on weight since arriving in Chile. My once trim build looked swollen, my face puffy, my clothes newly tight in places they hadn't been before. Without the money to cut or color my hair, my blonde curls had grown out into their natural mousy brown. It was uncomfortable to look at, let alone live in. To try to compose myself, I smoothed down my frizzy hair and took off Trey's soaking-wet jacket. I wished I had bought an umbrella and wondered why I hadn't thought to do so on my way. Once inside the office, I waited in the lobby and tried to appear as professional as I could, given the circumstances. Slight, beautifully put-together women with dark glistening hair and perfect complexions glided by. Each one amplified how disorganized and unfashionable I felt—like a hulking, disgusting American who had just smoked a wet cigarette in the pouring rain. After more than a few minutes of self-torture in the sparkling clean lobby, a woman named Rosa introduced herself and welcomed me back to the part of the office where the English class coordinators worked.

"This is Lindsey, Karen, and Cass," Rosa said, motioning to the three women who sat clicking away at computers in the tiny room. Each of the women swiveled their chairs around to face me, smiled, and introduced themselves.

"I'm Bree, nice to meet you," I said. "It's a little rainy out there," I joked, hoping that at the very least my sense of humor would endear me to them.

"Ha! No kidding! Girl, you're soaked," the woman with the long brown hair said smiling. I liked her. She was Lindsey.

"So let's talk about classes. You've been teaching English here with another institute, correct?" Rosa inquired.

"Yes. I'm enjoying them, but I'd like more. I have my ESL certification obviously, I brought it with me if you need to see it," I replied.

"And are you planning to stay here in Chile?" Rosa questioned.

"Yeah, my husband and I moved here in December and are building a house off the coast right now, but I plan to stay in Santiago as long as I need to for work," I said. Trey had just temporarily quit his job to focus on building the house but I wouldn't mention the fact that we were in financially dire straits.

"That's great," Karen chirped. She seemed more experienced than her youthful face gave her credit for. "We've got a big project coming up, that's why we brought you in today," she added.

"Would you be interested in an ongoing project? This opportunity is with the biggest airline in Chile. We just sold a program to them and have a large group of flight attendants who signed up for an intensive English-language course," she said. "The class would be here in Providencia—you'll have at least three or four classes a day. It will go for a few months, if not longer. Oh, and I almost forgot," she added. "The class pays 20,000 pesos an hour. Sam gave you a great recommendation. So what do you think?"

"Wow yeah, that sounds amazing," I replied. A consistent income at around forty dollars an hour? *This class could save us*, I thought.

"Great. Lindsey is designing the course, so she'll help you out with the specifics," Karen finished.

"Hey there," Lindsey said. "Come sit and I can show you the materials." She was warm, like all my favorite people. "So here are the course packets you'll cover with each class, each folder is marked here as well," she said, opening the rainbow-colored folders and flipping through the lesson plans. Each was meticulously organized and color-coded. "It should be easy to follow," she explained.

"Great, looks easy enough."

"And if you need anything, just let me know, okay? I'm always here to help or answer questions. That should be it! I'll walk you out," she said.

I collected my still-wet coat and bag and followed Lindsey to the hallway that separated the English area from the other offices.

"Where are you from?" I asked her, hoping to engage in small talk before I left and spent the rest of the day alone. Trey was at the property.

"Seattle, but I've been here for about eight years. I left once and came back, actually," she replied.

"Oh wow, that's awesome," I replied, trying not to sound too eager.

"Yeah, what about you?" she asked. "So you're building a house here? That's awesome."

"We're from Pennsylvania, and yeah, we just bought land outside Valpo, in a little beach town called Laguna Verde."

"Well why don't I give you my number, you have my email, if you ever want to hang out sometime," she said.

"Yeah definitely! We don't really know many people here yet. I'd love to have someone to drink wine with," I replied, obviously excited by the prospect of friendship. My cheeks flushed red.

"Oh for sure," she smiled, "That's one of my favorite things."

I didn't hesitate to call her, at first under the guise of work and later, to socialize. I had never been shy about meeting new people and Lindsey and I became fast friends. We were similar and our relationship felt easy, which was a welcome change in a situation that had become increasingly difficult. And she was generous with the life she'd built for herself in Chile.

I'd visit her one-bedroom apartment downtown near Plaza Italia. She always had wine and was happy to share since she understood that we had no money and she'd been there too, she explained. I'd bum Lucky Strikes, one after another, and we'd talk until 2 AM about our parents and our past and the things we wanted for our futures. We'd play our favorite music over a crappy laptop speaker and walk to the corner store for more cigarettes, more wine, and our favorite snack—a frozen pizza in the shape of an ice cream cone that after cooking stayed frozen in the middle but molten hot on the outside. We burnt our drunken tongues every time we ate them and laughed and danced to 90's music until we couldn't breathe. Our friendship made me feel like expat life could be fun, like I didn't just move to Chile to work my ass off. Lindsey introduced me to other American expats, like Kate and Alicia from Minnesota who also worked at the Institute, and there was Sam from Wisconsin, who I already knew. Lindsey had a Chilean boyfriend, Boris, and her two other best friends were Chilean women she'd known since the beginning of her time in Santiago, Carla and Jeimy. I was delighted to have a group of people again.

The days beat on, and our lives continued to revolve around the unifying goal of the house project, but further away from everything else. Making progress on the house was the priority, so out of necessity, Trey started teaching again and we packed our schedules with as many classes as we could. The majority of our paychecks went straight into the project for paint, floorboards, and wooden panels to build out the sides of the house. Since we didn't have access to a bank, our cash was organized in a little black binder we shoved under our mattress; after the cost of house supplies had been deducted, we were left with a weekly budget of about sixty dollars. We had to get creative in order to feed ourselves and the dog so we bought economy-size bags of rice to boil with cheap packets of instant soup and added as much salt and pepper as we could to give it flavor. We ate it for breakfast, lunch, and dinner for a week while we waited for our next monthly paycheck and Japhy gave up eating since he couldn't stomach any more of the bland mush on the menu.

That same week the Beast got broken into twice on our street in Santiago and lost her radio and then a window to theft. It didn't bother us much though, since we couldn't hear the music over her noisy engine anyway. Once the weather turned cold, our space heater broke and our landlord refused to fix it so we were forced to wear sweaters and scarves to bed at night. A week later our washing machine broke, so we ended up taking our dirty clothes to a woman in Laguna who would hand wash everything in a plastic bin outdoors for the equivalent of ten dollars. Nothing ever really got clean.

There was no more sipping espresso in the cafe near our apartment or walks to the pizza place on the corner. Eventually there was no more money or energy for anything Trey deemed superfluous, like a social life, or hobbies or a weekend off. Little by little, we were streamlining our focus. It seemed like the universe and Trey's vision conspired to whittle away the trappings of our old lives to make space for something new.

In between English classes he'd wrap himself in his blue cotton scarf and sit in a Starbucks to keep warm because they'd allow him to be there without buying anything but a small cup of black coffee. He'd sketch out the house plans on note cards and notebooks, measuring out the ways he'd have to cut corners to afford the next batch of lumber. And I'd count coins every morning, hoping I'd have enough to take the subway to work. When I didn't have enough to afford public transportation, I'd listen to music by Iron and Wine as I walked, pretending my life was a movie wherein I was the heroine and star—imagining myself as the protagonist of some great narrative, a hero's journey—to keep my mind off my homesickness.

I'd video call my best friend Kristen over the intermittent internet connection between English classes while I smoked cheap cigarettes on a bench, hidden amid the flower bushes outside my office building. Located among upper class residences, the outdoor seating offered me prime people-watching opportunities so instead of having lunch, I'd sit smoking with headphones in my ears. Short, stocky women wearing starched maid outfits walked little dogs, and stay-at-home moms carted children around the block. When I was able to connect with friends and family from back home, I fielded questions about the motivation behind our madness and tried to sound self-assured in our shared dream of a life off-grid. But maintaining faith in the project was a challenge, especially on an empty stomach with even emptier pockets. In less than a year we'd gone from a full life of friends and safety to a challenging foreign reality. It was so stark, the having and then the lack. The excesses of our past lives made the present feel especially empty of things.

In Laguna, heading into winter that year, the seasonal rains hadn't started yet, but we knew we were on borrowed time. We needed to get the roof up to protect the newly set floors and prevent the frame from swelling and warping. At that point, the house consisted of the pillars we had poured, two-by-fours, two layers of wooden planks that created a floor, and a few walls of plywood. Without power tools or the electricity available to power them, the work was slow and strenuous. Two-by-fours were cut with a hand saw and everything was held together by thick nails that Trey drove into each junction himself. If we didn't find a way to complete the roof, Trey would have to rip everything up and start over. In desperation, we started selling the last of our belongings that held any monetary value. We gathered up our favorite books we had brought from home, which sold quickly on a blanket on the street outside our apartment. The only other object that was worth anything was Trey's beloved Canon digital SLR camera, which he sold to a pawn shop downtown for just enough to buy the supplies we needed.

Trey was afforded a break from work in between job assignments so he committed to finishing the walls and roof of the house in the few weeks we assumed we had before the rains began. He loaded up the Beast with materials from the home improvement store in Valparaiso and spent the week building from sunup to sundown. He slept in the Beast with the dog because he was too exhausted to pitch a tent and came home to me in Santiago on the weekends to shower, wash his clothes, and get a break from his construction diet of beer and peanut butter sandwiches.

A few days into the work, he hired Carlos, a neighbor who was the unofficial security guard for the tiny sector of land between our house, Adrien's house, and Rosa and Ricardo's house. The roof would be all but impossible to construct alone so Trey asked him to lend a hand with construction, offering to pay him in installments—half before, and half after completion of the work. But when Carlos refused to work unless he received full pay upfront, Trey obliged, since we didn't know anyone else who could help him. On his first day of work, Carlos showed up late, carrying a box of wine; after one full day of work he disappeared with his full salary. He never returned to finish. Not wanting to burn any bridges (Carlos was one of the only people we knew who lived in Laguna full-time), we let the injustice go, but we promised ourselves we would think twice about trusting a stranger again. With no other options available, Trey finished the roof of the house alone with only a hammer and nails, just before the rains came to the coast.

My twenty-fifth birthday was approaching and as a birthday gift, my mom offered to pay for a plane ticket to return to Pennsylvania for a week. Nearly a year had passed since I had been home, but it felt like much longer and I was anxious to see everyone. Trey's parents offered to pay for his ticket too, but he declined. "Too much work to do," he said. So he stayed and I left.

I landed in summer, my favorite time of the year. As I departed the plane and stepped onto US soil I was overwhelmed with tears. I wiped my eyes with my shirt sleeve and looked up at the TV screen where a local news anchor was discussing the weather. Advertisements for cell phone providers blanketed the walls and I didn't recognize the song that was playing in the Hudson News where I grabbed a bag of Smartfood popcorn and a Vitamin water. I felt the same way I did the first time I returned home after leaving for college, like everything had changed in my absence. Everything seemed bigger than I had remembered—the highways, the people, the conveniences. And life had gone on without us. The five thousand miles that separated me from my friends and family had made keeping up with the minutiae of their lives nearly impossible, and being back made the distance feel more real than when I was away. I felt different, not just from them, but from the me I used to be. I tried my best to hide the toll the year of stress had taken, but my mom cried when she saw me. I was sure I looked about as ugly and tired as I felt.

My parents were still together, though it was obvious they would rather not have been. The house was still up for sale, too, and the real estate market in the States was so bad that no one was sure when or if they could sell the house they owned together. Maybe when it sold they would split up, but then what? Where would they go? I was pretty sure that my dad had been fired from his job, since instead of working he sat in the computer room all day watching YouTube videos. But they said nothing about their dwindling savings. In fact, they barely spoke to one another and when they did, their conversation was punctuated by jabs of nastiness and passive aggressive one-liners. It felt like being torn down the middle. They were too involved in the unraveling of their lives to question how I was handling my own so they asked about the superficial things, *How was work*, and *Have you made friends?* My brother made the trip home from college to see me. We all pretended that my parents divorce wasn't imminent by drinking massive amounts of vodka cranberries around the kitchen island. If everyone was drunk it was easier to ignore the obvious.

The week flew by and before I knew it, Trey's parents were hosting a party for me at the farm the day before my departure. Leaving again with the knowledge that it was most likely the last time I'd return to my childhood home made me feel empty. More than sad, I felt like I had lost my home in every sense of the word. Even my parents seemed like they no longer belonged to me. That night while our friends partied on the back porch, the scene of so many of our best memories together, I retreated to Trey's childhood room. I looked at the bookshelves, full of the stories and poems he had read to me when we first met. I remembered lying next to him in his twin bed, wondering what kind of woman I'd have to be to keep a man like him. I dialed his Chilean cell phone number and he picked up after the second ring.

"Everyone misses you," I said.

"That's not home anymore; this is my home now."

"I don't want to come back," I cried into the phone.

The other end of the line was silent. We had started to speak the truth, but there was a price we would pay for our honesty. Our project had just started and quitting would mean the end of more than just the house.

So I returned to Chile.

It was raining when I landed in Santiago and I watched the drops make pathways down the darkened airplane window, trying hard not to cry when the pit in my stomach demanded my attention. After the twelve-hour flight, I felt exhausted and numb, stuffed back into my old jeans with my summer sunburn newly peeling. I shuffled off the plane and into customs and threw the *US Weekly* tabloid magazine I had bought into the trashcan on my way past security. I spotted the Beast (it was hard to miss) waiting in the arrivals section with its lights flashing. I pried open the trunk and threw in my backpack and suitcase.

"Hey, how was the trip?" He offered once I sat down. The Beast smelled of sweat and earth.

His greeting felt like how you'd greet a stranger and seeing him gave me the same pit in my stomach I had felt sitting alone in his childhood room.

"Good," I said.

He gave me a perfunctory kiss.

"How have you been?" I asked.

"Busting my ass. Walls are up. Got a lot of work done. It started raining basically right after I finished up."

"Well, thanks. I'm sure it looks great. Everyone at home is good. They say hi, they miss you," I added.

"Yeah well, glad you had fun," he said disingenuously.

"Classes start next week again so I got as much done as I could while you were gone." He looked worn-down, or maybe annoyed, but I didn't have the energy to inquire more.

A few months passed and winter turned to spring. A day before our first wedding anniversary, we drove the noisy Beast to the home improvement store to buy windows for the house—a pivotal moment as it meant we could finally remove the plastic window coverings we had placed temporarily. We happily walked through the store, purchased windows in hand, thanking our lucky stars that our savings had materialized into something so important. But after we had bought the windows and loaded them into the car, Trey reached into the black money organizer that we kept with us at all times to count our change.

"Fuck." His hands searched the wallet frantically for our cash. "Fucking shit, you have to be kidding me."

Our money, the equivalent of about four hundred dollars, was nowhere to be found. In our haste to leave the store it must have fallen out of one of our pockets before we had returned it to the money organizer. We searched on hands and knees throughout the cement floor of the store for over an hour but it was no use—someone had scooped it up as quickly as we had dropped it. It was the only money we had for the rest of the month. I cried the entire ride home and he cursed, but none of that mattered.

In November we officially moved out of our apartment in Santiago and into the house in Laguna, which felt less like a house and more like camping; there was no plumbing, no electricity, and no interior walls. To complete the move, I transported the last of my personal belongings on the bus and Trey picked me up at the station (he had moved out the week before)—my old blue backpack on my shoulders. Halfway through the drive home I realized that I had left the container full of all my favorite jewelry in the overhead compartment of the bus. It had taken years to accumulate my prized collection of old baubles and vintage necklaces and special pieces from my travels—it was priceless and irreplaceable. But there was no use in going back to look for it. It was probably already stolen and really, I no longer wanted to call attention to myself with fancy, shiny things.

NEW NORMAL
February, 2011

I quickly descended the subway stairs near the Smart English office in Providencia. It was the end of my work week in Santiago, time to shape-shift again from city-dweller back to homesteader. I had gotten a promotion at the institute that required me to be in the office Mondays through Wednesdays, so during the week I stayed with Lindsey in her studio apartment, who generously let me do so rent free.

I took a deep breath and steadied myself for the trip I had ahead of me. The commute home required a train to the bus station, a ninety minute bus to Valpo, an hour-long *micro* to Laguna, then a mile walk to the unfinished house. The seventy-five mile journey took over four hours. Occasionally Trey would be running errands and could pick me up in town. Sometimes the sun was setting over the water as I'd descend into Laguna and I'd remember to appreciate how beautiful it was. Sometimes I wouldn't.

Living in Laguna was anything but comfortable, and the house was perpetually a work in progress. While we worked to save our pesos for a solar panel setup, the only electricity we had came from the solar-powered lantern we had brought with us from the States. Nights ended early without the ability to see past sundown. We showered, only occasionally, by using a black bag made of thick plastic that we filled with water and left in the sunshine to heat up.

I'd take my clothes off in the middle of the yard (there was no one watching anyway) and turn the bags's spigot, releasing a trickle of water through the hose while I soaped up my goose-bumped arms. My towel would inevitably fall in the dirt while I showered, but for the rest of the day I'd smell myself and be thankful for the soft, comforting scent of soap. Without a toilet, we relieved ourselves in holes we dug in the ground in the dense pine tree cover surrounding the property. I couldn't afford any makeup, skincare, shampoo. Sometimes when we ran out of toothpaste we'd go without. We stole toilet paper from wherever we could, usually from the university in Viña del Mar, where we had been teaching classes for a few months. We were stripped bare of everything. I didn't recognize myself and I don't think he recognized me either.

We had upgraded from a small hole in the ground for making our fire to a brick-lined pit, but cooking was still a time-consuming endeavor. Making coffee, for instance, was a process that took over an hour. Step one was to collect sticks from around the yard and find pieces of paper to serve as a fire starter. Then, we'd arrange sticks and paper in the perfect configuration to create a spark, prepared to re-do the arrangement multiple times if it failed to work the first time. Throw curse words to the foggy air. Fill the coffee pot with water from the only gallon of water left. Place the pot on the fire and hope it's hot enough to boil. Repeat the process whenever you want to eat or drink something warm. The hassle of cooking meant we kept meals simple. I got accustomed to eating as much as possible in one sitting since I never knew what the next meal would be.

We had bought a used foam mattress from an acquaintance in Laguna that ended up giving us fleas, but it was better than sleeping on the ground or in the car. Trey had placed foam insulation in as many walls as he could, but the floors were still plywood. They were always covered with a layer of dirt, but I kept sweeping anyway.

"This is so hard, Trey," I said as I cooked pasta over the fire; it was oftentimes the only thing we had to eat: cheap coffee and pasta with tomato sauce in single-serve packets.

"I know, Bree."

"I don't know if I can do this."

"Well, what the hell do you want to do?"

"I don't know, I love you," I said, as if he and the house were one and the same.

"I love you too, but I don't know how to make you happy."

"I need some creature comforts, a night out, friends, a night of fun with you like we used to do. Something." When I leaned into the ease of living with Lindsey in Santiago, I felt disconnected from Trey. The office job, a hot shower, grocery stores, friends. During the day my friends and I worked on English curriculum and at night, we'd hit happy hour—either the expat Irish bar or the balcony of one of their apartments. Our girls' nights were filled with music and wine and cigarettes, avocados and gossip and *ensalada chilena*. I contributed what I could. They were thoughtful and didn't ask questions when I couldn't share the cost of the night, but my lack of money was embarrassing.

If I voiced that side of me, the part that enjoyed normalcy, he'd remind me of the larger plan.

"All of those things will come when the house is done," he said.

"I should be able to enjoy myself once in a while."

"There is no should." It was one of his favorite sayings, delivered like a father who was course-correcting a child. Period, conversation over.

I eventually agreed that everything worth anything required hard work, suffering even, and so I came to view my discontent through the lens of the long game. *I may not be happy now*, I thought, *but some day my sacrifices will pay off.*

The seasons blended together in Laguna. Other than winter, when the rains dominated the forecast, the weather was temperate year-round. And because the seasons were flipped in the southern hemisphere, I couldn't rely on the usual markers to signify the passing of time. Christmas was in summer. I had a winter birthday. Fall was in April and Halloween was spring.

But summer finally came, hot and dry, and the house had taken the shape of a home, albeit a tiny one. At four hundred square feet, our entire living space was roughly the size of a two-car garage. A metal roof topped the A-frame structure and walls, which were natural wood because paint was too expensive. Inside, the floors were particle board and since we'd not yet placed insulation throughout, the walls were open to the studs. I'd use the spaces in between as if they were shelves, holding salt and pepper shakers and cigarettes. Trey had framed out the bathroom, which would eventually hold a toilet and a half-sized bathtub. A few pieces of drywall were strategically placed in what would become our bedroom. Constantly moving on to the next project, Trey worked quickly and planned everything out on little note cards that, just like his farming notes used to be, were strewn across the surfaces of our life. I helped with house projects in between teaching classes as much as I could, but he drove nearly every nail himself.

During a visit from friends, we had built a kitchen table out of scrap wood. It was so heavy it required two people to move, but it was functional, and it occupied the majority of the space that would become the kitchen at the back of the little house. There were two doors to the outside, one on the front of the house that served as our main entrance and another that led out to the backyard and faced the Pacific. On a clear day, you could see the faint blue outline of the ocean.

Outside, we had cleared our land of the little pine trees down to dusty dirt. Trey planted a lemon and a peach tree, plus a few flower bushes that he protected with small metal cages so wandering feral dogs wouldn't destroy them. He started work on the multi-chambered pit that would become the septic system and he'd dig for hours without stopping, covered in dirt with calloused hands. We had scraped together enough money to buy a white fiberglass tank that would one day live atop a metal tower and allow water to flow into the house; for now it sat empty on the ground.

In fall, I started living in Laguna full time. The institute where I worked in Santiago created a job for me in Valparaiso and gave me a full-time employment contract so I could get benefits like vacation time, bonuses, and a small but steady paycheck. But I was nervous about abandoning the security that my friends provided in Santiago. In Laguna, there were no distractions. There was no easy drive to a friend's house, or to a store, or to anywhere at all. But there was always work to be done. The project had taken on a life of its own. "The House," now a pronoun and a character in our lives just as important, if not more so, than I was. The full force of Trey's energy went toward advancing the house and I, with all of my extra needs for comfort and affection, was starting to feel like an unnecessary third wheel.

PROGRESS & PANIC
June, 2011

"No, no, no—Trey, turn around!" I tried to stay calm but they were starting fires all around us, throughout the length of Errazuriz street. The smell of burning tires permeated the flimsy truck windows.

The students had barricaded the main thoroughfare through town and now the riot police were retaliating.

"I don't know where else to go, Bree, we have to get through Valpo, class starts in an hour," he replied sternly.

"I know, but they're getting so close to us Trey—we shouldn't be here." Two masked students, or maybe they were simply protesters taking advantage of the chaos, threw rocks that hit the side of the Beast as we snaked through the only unblocked street. Another one held a Molotov cocktail—we had to move quickly.

"Oh shit," he said, as his eyes started to water. It had become a familiar feeling, the effects of the tear gas the police would employ to quell a protest: a tickle in your nose and then the sneezing would start. At that point, you knew you were already too close.

"Dammit, fucking *guanacos*," I said, pointing to the water cannons the police had begun using. For the last few months we had become skilled in the vocabulary of protest. "*Encapuchados* again, too." The sight of the masked protesters, *encapuchados*, meant things were about to escalate. While some protests had been peaceful, the situation throughout the country had started to deteriorate. But the students were holding their ground.

Working in both private education and at a public university, we were privy to both sides of the argument. The tenets of the student protests seemed sound: increase the quality and funding of public education and stop for-profit education. Simple enough in theory, but in practice, Chile was a country built on the ideals of neo-liberal capitalism with the US as its template. Even with the majority of the country in agreement with the requests, it would take sweeping and costly legislation to make a real impact. The demonstrations were becoming more violent as the students' demands went unmet, and *Presidente* Sebastián Piñera, a Harvard-educated conservative, was losing approval.

The protests and marches colored everything that winter. It seemed fitting though, that the chaos on the streets matched the chaos in my head.

The panic attacks I had identified a year before were getting more frequent. Nothing I did seemed to help. Every physical space felt too small to hold me and my anxious mind. Grocery stores were far too bright and *why hadn't I noticed before that they didn't have windows?* My heartbeat would quicken while I scanned the aisles for the closest exit. Waiting in bank lines, a frequent activity for an expat who was often paid by check, felt like torture. I could sense everyone staring at me as I rehearsed, over and over like a mantra, the words and phrases I'd say in Spanish to the cashier. "*Solo un deposito*," I'd say, feeling my hands turn sweaty. I rushed from one place to the next, feeling the need to escape to safety but with nowhere to go that actually felt safe. Some weekends I'd desperately want to retreat to Santiago with my friends so I didn't have to live in the house project—but not wanting Trey to feel betrayed by my leaving him there alone, I wouldn't.

Instead, I'd lie in bed, terrifying thoughts sliding into my head, taking up residence there. The longer they stayed, the more they seemed to grow. The more I tried to force them out, the stronger they became. I started wondering if there was a way I could just stop feeling things at all. I fell asleep most nights wishing I could opt out of everything, sleep through the next few months, or years, and wake up in a different life. Leaving Chile didn't feel like an option, but staying didn't either. I figured I had no resources to alter my situation, and was exhausted by the prospect of another change. I was ashamed at how quickly I had spiraled into a person who looked and felt nothing like the me I thought I was.

Trey continued to work with fervor on the house. Drywall went up in the hallway, the bathroom, and our tiny bedroom. He salvaged skinny wooden planks from an abandoned plot of land across the *quebrada* and used half of them to create a reclaimed wood ceiling for the bathroom. He used the other half to build out the underside of a breakfast bar he constructed in the kitchen. We saved every cork from the bottles of red wine we consumed to adorn the outside of our bathtub as decoration. We bought a bathroom sink, tiled the floor with slate, and installed a light fixture so we could stop peeing in the dark. He constructed cabinets and drawers for the kitchen and topped them with a butcher's block counter top, then we painted the cabinets white to brighten up the space. He built us a bed and used more reclaimed wood from the property across the way to add character. He built a bookshelf into a wall in the hallway to hold our books so they no longer had to sit in piles under the bed, collecting dust. A humble solar-powered electric setup was installed and he placed light switches in the kitchen and bedroom. We were careful not to waste even a moment's worth of electricity, since it took so long to fill the solar battery and was so easily drained.

Unlike long summer days, the winter weather challenged our homesteading way of life. Torrential downpours for days on end without sun to fill the batteries meant no electricity for the house. More, the frequent intense storms would flood the unpaved roads of upper Laguna Verde, which kept us on house arrest for days, running inside and out to chop logs to stoke the fire. So we reverted to old behaviors like charging cell phone batteries in public places and turning the lights off at sundown.

A few months later we were able to save up enough money to add another battery and more solar panels to amp up our simple electric system, which allowed Trey to install an electrical socket in the wall for charging our phones. If we got lucky with enough sun to fill the battery, we could watch a streaming movie on the clunky laptop my parents had bought me after my college graduation five years before. But the only internet we had access to was from a cheap USB internet stick, so we were more likely to get frustrated halfway through streaming than to watch the entire thing.

We bought a faux leather love seat that we should have tested in-store, as it turned out to be the most uncomfortable couch in history. Nonetheless, we were thankful to have somewhere cushioned to sit that wasn't a camping chair. We even bought a television and a dish that we affixed to the roof to catch a few cable channels. Most of the programming was overdubbed in Spanish but occasionally we'd land on a show that streamed in English and relished the chance to relax in the easy entertainment.

Living in a house that was perpetually under construction required an open mindedness about mess. No matter how often I swept and dusted, there was a layer of dirt covering every surface. Trey tried his best to keep things organized but it was nearly impossible to segregate the area that was in construction from the rest of the house. So construction materials, tools, and trash piled up and spilled into every nook and cranny, overtaking our living space.

Trey had created a basic plumbing system within the house and hooked up the large fiberglass tank to allow water to flow to our sinks. His ingenuity eventually gave us running water—albeit limited to the amount available in the tank—with which we could wash our dirty dishes or fill a pot of water to boil. Since the water from our tank wasn't drinkable, at the beginning of every week we'd purchase as many jugs of drinking water as we could, hoping to get through the week without a second trip to the store in town. We cooked every meal on the wood stove, which took some getting used to. The fire had to be strong enough and hot enough to cook anything and you had to monitor it closely. But after a while, I learned how and when to feed the flames. Like most things in our off-grid life, it required patience and presence. Trey eventually installed a solar-powered electric pump and point-of-use water heater so that instead of scrubbing ourselves in the bath with water heated on the wood stove, we could clean ourselves with a shower head. It was far from a normal-sized shower since we had nowhere to hang the shower head, and cleaning ourselves meant sitting in the bathtub and dangling the shower head above our heads, but it got the job done. Because it was uncomfortable, we showered only as frequently as was necessary.

"I should be able to enjoy a shower, creature comforts. I miss those things," I'd say on the hard days. I would have done anything for a hot bath or a normal anything at the end of a long work day.

"There is no should."

Though we lived paycheck to paycheck, watching our money go directly to tangible things for the house was satisfying. We measured our progress in nails, in drywall, in insulation. Success was a working toilet purchased on Christmas day, a septic system he dug himself, and a mattress without fleas on a frame he'd built. Progress looked like the four-burner wood stove made of white enamel and the realization that we no longer had to cook our meals outdoors. We took one step forward and another step back—two beers out at a bar, then two weeks of dry pasta for every meal. A solar panel in hand meant no money for gas for the car. It was always give and take, inching forward.

We did less complaining than the previous year. At least we had a wood stove, and we were thankful for the abundant wood that somehow stayed dry under the tarp outside. We counted our blessings for the hearty soup fixings we were smart enough to buy in advance of the storms. We were grateful for the bottle of red wine to share over the books our parents had mailed as gifts. The package they sent had arrived quickly, which was a miracle in itself. We'd lie in bed, listening to the rain beating off the metal roof. But we never stayed comfortable for long.

The Beast broke down and we were left without a vehicle for nearly three weeks during which heavy rains pummeled the entire coast. Walking home from the bus in the rain every night, flashlight in hand, wearing a bright orange jumpsuit to stay dry, I had to laugh. It felt like life was testing us. It was relentless. One morning we accidentally left our bedroom window open and came home to find that our entire savings had been stolen from the hiding place on the wooden shelf Trey had built to hold our sweaters. We installed bars on our windows.

Trey and I argued as much about small things as we did the big things. I'd poke and prod.

"I need you to tell me I'm beautiful," I'd say, especially on the days I knew affection was the last thing on his mind. I wanted to press him, if only to prove my point that he was wrong. "You know I need certain things from you."

"And I, you," he'd return. "I need you to help me with the house more. I've been working my ass off alone on this. I've pounded every nail."

Our little house had become a pressure cooker. It was hard for us to find comfort in anything, including one another. And while we danced in circles around each other, always returning to the same argument, I still trusted him, the project, and my place within the life we were creating. The only thing between us and a happy ending was the work, I thought. Our salvation was in persevering.

So we pressed on, maybe more out of stubbornness than hope, with the expectation that someday we would look back from the other side.

SOCIAL LIFE
November, 2011

I had always kept a large group of friends. People felt comfortable, and comforting. But they were also a way to escape myself. If I kept myself busy looking outward, I could focus my attention on how I was perceived, rather than how I felt. Trey was different, or at least I thought he was. He had friends, of course, but most felt unnecessary—disposable, even. Living in solitude in Laguna was perfect for a man like him. But for me, living in Launga without my usual means of distraction or coping mechanisms meant that I felt deeply uncomfortable a lot of the time.

He'd call me "party girl," when I expressed a need to go out, or take time off from the house project. He'd tell me how unnecessary it all was—socializing, parties, the sharing of space and time. A social life was a thing I was made to feel needy for wanting, like I hadn't stripped myself bare enough yet; that the optimal state for a person was to be free of the trappings of normalcy, whatever that meant. While I agreed with Trey about the necessity of ridding oneself of habits that no longer served you, it was confusing to both believe him and also miss people so much I could barely function.

So I did what any lonely extrovert expat would do and started striking up conversation with anyone who crossed my path: in the study hall at the university, at the corner store in town, at the bus stop waiting for the *micro*; anywhere was a good enough place to meet someone new. I took it upon myself to build a community. I even joined a Facebook group created for expats who lived near us, in the fifth region of Chile. Many of the expats in Valparaiso and neighboring Viña del Mar were women from other countries who had married Chileans and installed themselves into Chilean life. The rest were mostly students or young professionals, like us, who had fallen in love with Chile and stayed. There was a small but tight-knit group of expats in the region and I was eager to find my place within it.

There was Susan, a mother of two from the Midwest who had been an English teacher for over a decade. Stef and Brian were on sabbatical from their lives in San Francisco. Peter and Ben ran a tourism company together and lived in a creaky old house at the top of a hill in Valpo. And then there was Sammi. Sammi was an American, though she'd been living in Chile for nearly two decades and was more or less the social director of the entire group. She understood everything there was to know about navigating the system in Chile, like the steps to renew your visa and how to do your taxes or the idiosyncrasies of the Chilean people. When she wasn't busy running the restaurant she owned with her husband or teaching classes, she baked bagels for those of us who were missing that particular creature comfort from back home. She was a mother hen to all of us who lacked and missed our own mothers, or at least that's how I felt about her. Everyone knew Sammi. And becoming her friend made me feel like I was part of the unique cohort of expats who could appreciate Chile enough to want to stay long-term.

And in Laguna, our next door neighbors Adrien and Violeta started living at their off-grid home full-time. Violeta was perfectly suited for the homesteading lifestyle. She was relaxed, resourceful, and hard-working and I was thankful to have her companionship. We quickly, and out of shared necessity for a social connection, became each other's closest female companions. I'd march down the path through the pines in beat-up UGG boots with two glasses of wine to share and we'd shoot the shit about life in Laguna. Some nights we'd share a joint and spend our time smoking and laughing on their outside patio in sheep's wool sweaters she had brought back home from Chiloe in the south. She made me feel less alone.

Adrien and Violeta were adept at making friends and *pitutos*, networks of connections throughout Laguna and Valpo that came in useful when something needed to get done. Adrien knew who to call for the cheapest gravel delivery or the fastest repair for a broken water heater. They introduced us to new friends too, like Maria and Victor, a couple with twin boys who had moved to Laguna to escape from city life. Maria taught yoga and offered an hour-long class every Tuesday in the community center that Trey and I started to attend every week. I had only ever dabbled in yoga but after a few months of classes, I started to notice changes in the way I approached my days, with more patience for everything. Yoga gave me a sense of belonging with the other people in class. And devoting time to something together outside of the House every week felt like a breath of fresh air for our relationship. We didn't rush to class or complain about Chile when we were there. The hour and a half we allotted to doing yoga created a space between us where we could talk about something besides the project and simply be together. Our classes soon became my favorite part of the week. With other people propping us up, life in the Chilean countryside started to feel less scary.

As our group of friends grew, so did our opportunities to spend time enjoying ourselves. Occasionally, I'd convince Trey to leave the ever-present work at home and venture out to have some fun, though getting anywhere outside of Laguna took at least forty-five minutes.

One temperate summer night, Peter and Ben invited us to their house on Cerro Polanco, which was a revolving door of expats and the hip cohort of Chileans who congregated there. We pulled up to the house on the hill in the Beast, the engine sputtering again. Trey cursed its failing parts as he slammed the door shut.

"I don't even know why we came out, this is the last thing I feel like doing."

I said nothing, climbed out of the car, pried open the metal gate into their courtyard, and stomped the mud from my boots onto the cement patio. I heard the faint laughter of people inside and fixed a smile on my face. Unlike Trey, I was thankful for the momentary distraction from the project.

Halfway through the evening I snuck away from the crowd to refill my empty wine glass. The smoke from the BBQ wafted into the open windows of the kitchen as I scanned the old house—the heavy wooden doors, the avocados on the counter—while outside the last of the day's sun blanketed the hills in orange. I wondered if there was anywhere else in the world that felt like Valparaiso—it was so different from all the other places I'd ever been. Regaetton blared on the speakers in Peter's room and the sound of laughter echoed down the hall. I turned and Ben's bedroom caught my eye. I inched closer and peeked in, made sure I was alone, then flicked on his light switch. *How nice*, I thought, as I stared at his fluffy twin bed. How comfortable it must feel to fall into it at the end of the night, alone or otherwise, and in the morning wake up to make breakfast or enjoy a quick walk to a cafe. He could do whatever he wanted, go anywhere, be with anyone. A silent jealousy bubbled up inside of me as I stared at the folded clothing in his open drawer and thought about the clean, working bathroom down the hall.

Was I missing out on something?

At the end of the night, Trey and I jumped in the Beast, hoping it would start, then crept noisily through the empty streets of Valparaiso, through the tunnel so thick with fumes I had to hold my breath, and finally up the hill back home. The life of the city faded away the further we drove and soon, I could smell Laguna's telltale eucalyptus trees through the drafty windows. I looked up at the black sky dotted with glittering stars, then stared in silence at the unlit road ahead. It was just the two of us—me and the man to my left, who was busy shifting gears with a head full of plans.

CAR TROUBLE
January 2012

I lit the cheap cigarette and took an exaggerated drag—it tasted awful but we couldn't afford Lucky Strikes anymore—then closed my eyes in the passenger seat. To my left Trey was steering as cautiously as he could, doing his best to keep the Beast between the edge of the cliff and away from oncoming traffic, while a rope tethered our front bumper to the mechanic's truck in front of us. The Beast had died again, this time on the stretch of road between Playa Ancha and Laguna. We were thankful to have finally found a mechanic in town reliable enough to call in a pinch, but due to this latest setback we found ourselves slowly traversing the side of a mountain with nothing between us and certain death but a thick rope and the steady hands of a Chilean mechanic named Richard. He had assured us this was the way they did things here and the rope would hold. "Just take it easy and steer," he advised, so I hopped in the passenger seat with Trey at the wheel, praying to God that we would make it down the coast to safety. When we did make it, unscathed but shaking with adrenaline and nerves, I didn't know whether to be grateful or angry.

Our car problems had started out benign enough but had grown worse by the month, then worse after that, and while Trey was skilled in house-building, he was no mechanic. And since we needed the truck to get to work every day, we sought repairs wherever we could find them. Occasionally, the auto repair shops we found were honest, but most of the time they took advantage of two gringos with little to no knowledge of cars (or Spanish automobile vocabulary) who were urgently looking for a fix for their rusty old truck. We once paid the equivalent of eight hundred dollars for someone to replace a silicone seal on an oil pan. Another mechanic promised he had fixed our brakes, but they failed just days later.

Not having a reliable vehicle added another strain to our already-tense living situation. The Beast was far from a luxury ride but it definitely beat the long walk to the bus stop, down the dusty dirt trail we had originally traversed on our first trip to the land. We were regularly stranded at bus stops across the fifth region, waiting for a bus that, coincidentally, had just left. If the errand, or job, or event wasn't absolutely necessary, we wouldn't attend. I felt the isolation of our house more acutely. And the expense of constant auto repairs made other things, like advancing the house, impossible.

But then we met Richard. Richard was a silver-haired mechanic who lived in town in a house with a terracotta roof and a succulent garden his wife kept in meticulous order. I never saw him wearing anything other than a gray jumpsuit splattered with car oil, and his thick hands were always stained with a layer of grease. We had plenty of work to give him and we soon found out that his fixes actually worked, unlike those of the other mechanics we had hired. He seemed to take pity on two expats with a geriatric automobile and little cash—and thankfully, he was resourceful. Given that our truck was almost thirty years old and the correct parts were virtually non-existent, instead of denying us service or suggesting we ditch the old Beast, he substituted in parts from other vehicles. It was a relief to realize that we could rely on him. He eventually earned our trust, which was pretty much all we had to offer. But on the way home from work one day, the Beast finally broke down for good. In a dramatic ending befitting her long life, her engine fell out of her body while we were traveling the road into town. If it weren't so awful it would have been hilarious.

So we saved up more money, bought another unreliable vehicle, procured a Chilean credit card and eventually found ourselves the owners of a fully-functioning Toyota Rav 4. Our new ride, which purported to get us where we were going without having to worry about the wheels falling off or the engine blowing up, was a panic-attack-free vehicle. The car was a game changer. It also meant that I no longer had the excuse of a broken vehicle to explain why I didn't want to drive in Chile.

Somewhere along the way, I had become terrified of driving. It may have been the unreliable cars, the unfamiliar roads, my peaking anxiety, or a combination of all three, but either way, since we arrived in Chile I had flat out refused to drive anywhere. Months earlier, I had reluctantly learned how to drive a manual transmission and now it was time for me to shoulder the responsibility of driving too.

Driving around our little town was easy enough, so long as it wasn't raining and the dirt roads weren't flooded out, but leaving Laguna was another story. That drive required we travel the only route out of Laguna, which was a skinny two-lane road carved into the coastline. I was rattled with nerves every time we traveled it, even as a passenger. And the fun didn't stop there. Once you had successfully reached the summit, the next step on your journey to Valpo or Viña was either through Playa Ancha, where stop-and-go traffic and reckless micro drivers were the norm, or you could go directly into Valparaiso via La Polvora, a high-speed highway that twisted back and forth between the ocean and the hills and was almost permanently occupied by a dense fog in the cooler months. Our road companions on La Polvora were cargo trucks that rushed into Valpo's port, heavy with red and orange international transport crates, and random puttering automobiles, either creeping slowly up the side of the road or speeding along carrying cargo tied to the roof. As a newbie manual-driver, I wasn't sure which route was worse. Even when Trey was at the wheel, my imagination became a movie screen that I couldn't turn off, showcasing vividly real and epic car crashes. To protect myself on such a treacherous stretch of road, I became hyper vigilant, as if by imagining every scary scenario I could somehow avoid them through careful and strategic preparation. Regardless of my fear, I couldn't continue to ask Trey to be my chauffeur.

So one morning, heart pounding in my chest and palms sweating, I decided it was time to force myself to drive to class. I waved goodbye to Trey and Japhy and flung my work bag into the passenger seat. I shifted into reverse, creeping slowly out of our dirt driveway, then into first, and second, as I wound down the worn path towards town, feeling a mix of curiosity and alarm at the fact that I was alone. I hadn't driven anywhere alone for years. I gained speed as I cruised past the bus stops and eucalyptus and up the *cuesta*, looking down at my sweating hands leaving wet marks on the gray plastic steering wheel and watching a green and orange micro fly down the side of the hill and whoosh past my window.

Holy shit, I was doing it.

I merged onto La Polvora and took a deep breath, then shifted into fourth gear. Out of the corner of my eye I noticed the Pacific to my left, peeking out from above the concrete. I could see the white-capped waves in the distant blue. I remembered a familiar feeling from my pre-Chile life—freedom—and realized how much I missed solo driving. Minutes and miles passed quickly and after awhile I exited the highway and slowed to take in the view—an old lighthouse, a cemetery, a naval building. I flipped on the radio to play the only CD we owned, *Bob Marley's Greatest Hits*, and cranked the window down to let in the ocean air. I caught my eye in the rear-view mirror and recognized myself for the first time in a long time.

There you are, I thought.

I had done another thing that frightened me; I had pushed through the discomfort. I walked to class with a light step, smiling, my teacher's bag bouncing at my side.

A SWIMMING POOL

February, 2012

Two years into building we were still plugging away at the house. Our progress was slow because we never made much money, so we were constantly trying to find ways to make more. For two summers we worked at a cruise ship check-in, alternating between speaking English and Spanish and fumbling with international passports. We gave tours and took tourists to wine tastings at a fancy vineyard in the *Zona Central* that specialized in Sauvingnon Blanc. Trey built chairs and I bought American name-brand clothing to sell to college students at the university. Trey hated leaving our land and was convinced that if he spent enough time on his own projects, we wouldn't have to rely on extra work to survive, whereas I thought working overtime would be the key to our financial success. We argued a lot.

That summer, a friend of Trey's offered him construction work at an off-the-grid property in a town called Tiltil, about an hour and a half inland. He begrudgingly accepted the work to fund the completion of our porch and maybe even outfit a new greenhouse. Though it wasn't luxurious, I couldn't wait for the opportunity to camp out in a new place for a few weeks.

We hit the road, traveling north through Viña del Mar, then east across Olmue, into the agricultural region along Ruta 60, which cut through countryside farms where avocados, grapes and the famous *limachino* tomatoes grew under thick greenhouse plastic. Rustic-looking homes dotted both sides of the road with terracotta roofs, signs outside advertised hefty bags of oranges in mesh bags piled high. The coastal fog lifted as we traveled further east, until the increasing peaks of the cordillera were visible in the distance. Before we knew it, the mountains were all around us and we were on Cuesta la Dormida, one of the more famous roads in Chile. *Cuesta,* in Spanish, means a road that climbs a hill and Cuesta la Dormida is the trail that traverses the beginning of the Andes, or the end of them, depending on which way you look at it. The hills that marked the start of the Andes were stacked one behind the other like dominoes, each one grander than the first. And since the coastal breeze couldn't reach us there, it was much hotter than we were used to. Chile's geography is wildly varied along its 2,653-mile length but since we hadn't traveled much, it was easy to forget how diverse the landscape and the climate really was. We continued twisting through the arid desert switchbacks until I checked the map our friend had painstakingly drawn for us and confirmed we were close. A dust storm flared directly in front of our car, twisting and picking up dry branches in its swirl, and by the time we arrived, it felt like I had been gifted a new set of eyes. Chile didn't look or feel the same here.

That night, Trey and I found ourselves atop the hill, where we had set up our tent among the trees and construction, the moon above shining bright enough to light up the entire valley below us and bouncing off the peaks of the cordillera. The air felt almost like home with its hot summer nights on the farm. We hadn't had much dinner so I ripped open a bag of fancy potato chips and we passed them back and forth, licking the tangy dust off our fingertips. I could hear Japhy snoring quietly as gas generators churned in the distance. I turned to face Trey and he grabbed my hand and kissed me.

"This is nice," I said.

Our days in Tiltil were long and hot and after one day of

watching the men work, I decided I had better things to do with my time. I took the new car and got busy exploring. I stopped at the closest fruit stand and picked up watermelons and cantaloupe with Japhy in the passenger seat, stretching my independence, feeling like a happy, cool expat. My days had no agenda, so I would read a book for a while until the tent became too hot a place to relax, then venture into an opening in the woods where the eucalyptus trees surrounded the *parcela*. About a week into the project, the crew decided to take a day off, which afforded Trey and me a day to ourselves. A wide open day was a luxury we weren't often afforded and I was determined to fill it with something fun. I had passed what looked to be a public pool on my drives through Tiltil, so that morning I pitched Trey the idea of a swim. As a competitive swimmer during childhood all the way through college, I'd spent more hours in the pool than I could count. But since community pools were few and far between in Chile, I hadn't stepped foot in one since we had arrived years earlier. So on the first free day in what felt like a lifetime, I threw two old bath towels into the car, then hopped in the driver's seat and we set off toward the pool.

Unlike most of my time spent driving to and from home in Laguna, in Tiltil I appreciated the scenery. With no schedule or students waiting or bus to catch, I appreciated the rolling hills, the color of earth crisscrossing in front of us, decorated with patches of evergreen *litre* bushes whose oval-shaped leaves were known to cause allergic reactions, and the sporadic cactus. I wasn't even annoyed by the hot plastic seat sticking to my thighs. I cranked up the volume on the radio and sang along to Bob Marley since I now knew every word to every song on the *Greatest Hits Album*. After we bounced into an empty pool parking lot, throwing up dust in our wake, I threw on the e-brake and we optimistically made our way to the front of the building. A young guy manning the gated entrance fiddled with a deck of cards.

"How much is the entrance fee?" I asked.

"Two pesos a person," he answered.

"Holy shit Trey, it's cheap and open!" I couldn't believe our luck. By the time he paid the man I was already sprinting through the women's locker room. "Meet you on the other side!" I yelled through the brick partition.

I knew better than to run across a pool deck but I couldn't help it. With the excitement of a kid on Christmas morning, I grabbed one foot to pry off my plastic flip flop, bouncing on the other foot to maintain momentum, then switched legs and flung both flip flops in the air toward an empty plastic pool chair. I breathed in the smell of fresh air and chlorine. *God how I've missed this*, I thought. It was nothing fancy, a rectangular pool surrounded by a chain link fence and two locker rooms, but it felt special. The pool was my happy place. I peeled off my running shorts and t-shirt and jumped into the deep end without testing the water.

The cold water hit my hot skin and I sank to the bottom. I was ten years old again, and fifteen, and twenty. I was me again and I was home. I felt the bottom with my feet and looked around, eyes open without goggles like a quiet meditation. No matter where I was, the bottom of a pool always felt the same to me. I did a somersault on my way to the surface.

"Trey it's awesome!" I shouted across the pool to him when I noticed he had joined me. We had the entire place to ourselves.

"I'll come in in a minute, let me heat up," he returned.

I floated on my back and looked up at the big blue cloudless sky.

When I had my temporary fill of being in the water I jumped out and plopped myself on a plastic lawn chair facing what seemed to be a snack bar. *Snacks* was written across a flimsy plastic sign hanging crookedly above the counter. I didn't get my hopes up—we had learned not to after one too many a snack stop disappointment—but I wrung out my sopping-wet hair and hustled over to check out the selection anyway.

After quickly reading the menu written on a chalk board I realized they had flavored ice so I ran back over to Trey, bursting with the good news, and asked for a few *luka* to buy us some. He always held onto the cash, which was a responsibility I was happy to avoid. When I returned, I ordered a cherry ice and a plastic cup of beer for Trey. We picked a tiny table with an umbrella to savor our cool beverages and looked around.

"I actually love it here. If I could do this all the time, I'd be happy," I said, sloshing the slushie around in its plastic cup.

"I like it here too. What do you like about it?" Usually our conversations around Chile started off innocently enough but then devolved into me listing all of the ways life there was so hard for me. I would end up in tears and he'd end up stomping away—sometimes my tears came first and sometimes his dramatic exit did. Either way, I wanted to avoid that familiar territory, so I tried to stay positive.

"Well the heat is nice, and it doesn't feel so secluded—it feels... normal."

"Yeah I get it. I know Laguna is different from that and hard for you, I get it."

"I just don't know what to do Trey, we've put so much work into this already. I'm not saying we should go back to the States, I just..."

"Anywhere we go will be hard, maybe not as hard as this has been, but hard in ways we just don't know yet. I don't know if you'll be happy anywhere that isn't home."

"I'd like to try. I am trying. I'm doing the best I can."

I poked the red ice at the bottom of the cup, then poured the remainder of the sticky sweetness into my mouth in one shot.

"I know you are. We both are."

He seemed like he was listening to me, not just waiting to speak. So I did the same. Maybe we could communicate differently than we always had.

The next morning, before the heat hit, I went for a run. Running had become my release, my way outside of my anxiety, a mental break I so desperately needed. I threw my headphones in and trod down the bank, then past the gate and onto the pavement, where I jogged for a few miles along the country road. Beads of sweat trickled down my freshly freckled nose. I felt the familiar rush of endorphins as I returned back to our camp panting and covered in red dust up to my knees.

"Good run?" Trey asked as I hiked up the hill and into view.

"Sweaty and nice. All good here?"

"Making progress," he said, patting my leg affectionately as I made my way by.

I retreated into the woods to shower off my run. Once I found a suitably private spot, I hung our black shower bag on a low branch, propped up my sweaty phone next to it and pressed play on the music app I had downloaded. As soon as the notes hit the air, my mindset shifted. It felt like taking a giant step out of the present moment and seeing myself from above, or from the future, from a place with perspective. The shower in the woods, the running, the building, the difficulties—they were all pieces in the puzzle of our life. A life we had created from scratch. Sure, I was still lonely, money was always tight, and living off the grid was seriously hard in just about every way, but those things were just challenges. I could re-frame my experience if I tried hard enough. Maybe every moment was a test and every trial was a step toward the finish line. I didn't know exactly where the finish line was, but I knew we were closer than before. I sang along to the words of a song I'd been playing on repeat: *I could say I hope it will be worth what I give up.* I finished my shower and looked out through the fragrant leaves onto the valley below, a muted stretch of desert with only a handful of modest homes with tin roofs and chicken coops. I wrapped a tiny towel around my midsection, quickly found my way to the tent and in minutes the heat had evaporated the water from my arms. Trey and the crew must be taking a break, I thought, since there was quiet all around, save the bark of a distant dog and a rooster whose crow was hours too late. Japhy limped over to me. His legs had been bothering him more lately, and we sat together, hot and happy inside our little blue tent.

On our return trip to Laguna we stopped at a restaurant and filled ourselves with *chorrillana* (a meaty, salty, greasy plate of pure comfort food atop a bed of French fries) and two cold beers. Reggaeton played softly over the stereo while we sat together on a large outdoor couch facing a fire pit. I watched him while he sipped his cold beer and realized I couldn't remember the last time I had actually seen him. His messy blonde curls were long again since he insisted upon cutting his own hair and only did it when it was absolutely necessary. The lines around his eyes had gotten deeper in the way that happened to men who'd spent the majority of their lives outdoors, but it only served to make him more handsome. His hands were covered in sticky foam insulation that had now turned black, so I snapped a picture of them for posterity and noticed he actually looked happy. I settled into the couch's fluffy cushions, sipped my beer, then turned my attention back to him. For the moment, he wasn't distracted by work or angry that I was unhappy or rushing somewhere he didn't want to go. And sitting there on the couch with him, I wasn't lonely or missing something or longing to be somewhere else. He looked up from his beer, his gaze soft, and we locked eyes, seeing one another for what felt like the first time in a long time.

"I love you," I said.

"I love you too."

SPRING
September, 2012

The sun was shining underneath the wooden door; I opened it and made my way to one of the Adirondack chairs Trey had made. There wasn't a cloud in the sky. I had heard there was a hole in the ozone here, directly above us. I closed my eyes and felt the warm rays on my eyelids then took a sip of hot coffee. I loved mornings like this, slow and easy. Trey wasn't exactly the relaxing type, but even he had slowed down recently, our projects naturally shifting from necessities like running water and electricity to creature comforts. Our house no longer felt like a construction zone—in fact, it was starting to feel more like home. We had four walls, a bed, and a bathroom. We had all we needed.

We were changing too. We began to feel gratitude during simple moments when we were able to enjoy the fruits of our labor. Sitting on the couch in our warm house we owned without a mortgage, we felt the significance of what we had done. We built in ourselves an appreciation for energy, for every drop of water, for every easy flick of a light switch. Things that were once normal had become luxury, never to be taken for granted again. Even on the hard days, which were fewer, we always came back to the progress we had made.

"Look where we are."

"See what we've accomplished."

"We're always moving forward."

"Look at what we're doing Bree. Look at the big picture," he'd remind me. "Look how far we've come."

I got up early and cut logs for the fire. I started writing. I tried to stay present. Begrudgingly, I continued to push the boundaries of the things I thought I was capable of. There was no other choice. The person I was when I came to Chile was gone and in her place was a new someone I was just getting to know. I had changed in ways that I couldn't yet articulate.

Our constant toiling had started to pay off; all we had to do was look around to appreciate it. The land surrounding the house was no longer a dusty piece of dirt; it was lush with greenery and abundant with new life. We planted a garden bed full of *docas,* a native coastal plant with bright purple flowers, to line the front of our *parcela.* In case of a forest fire, which were unfortunately common throughout the region, we hoped the water-filled succulent would provide protection. The *tabaco del diablo* he had transplanted around the perimeter of the house had grown tall, its broad green leaves creating a natural green and orange border around the remainder of our property's exterior. He drove inland to a nursery to buy starter plants of artichokes, blueberries, and hydrangeas that we planted on the hill overlooking the steep *quebrada,* then carved out footpaths around the plantings to make watering them easier. The salty air and sea breeze had killed most of the unprotected and fragile little seedlings we planted the year prior, so Trey constructed a greenhouse that we could see from the kitchen window. We celebrated when the little shoots of salad greens and tomatoes burst through the soil.

I found that I preferred landscaping to house-building, maybe because it reminded me of the farm work that I missed, or maybe because the results came quicker and with less investment. I could spend hours cleaning up a hillside or a special little piece of our land, or creating a secret garden out of sticks and weeds and an overgrown *litre* bush. Unlike the brute force required of construction, uncovering the natural beauty of the place was easy.

And now that we had steady funds for food, cooking at home became a source of comfort. Trey built a pizza oven where the old brick fire pit used to sit, on the westernmost edge of the property, and we learned how to make our own pizza dough. We followed a recipe from the big red cookbook, measuring out flour, warm water, and yeast. I loved the simplicity of it—how the yeast was alive, and how the climate of Laguna affected the quality of the dough. Over time we worked on our recipe, shifting the ratios and cook times, the heat in the oven and the amount of salt. We'd each make one little pie, or two if we were extra hungry, like the personal pan pizzas from our childhood. I'd pile on fresh basil and veggies from our garden while he added pepperoni and extra cheese. After a while, the brick oven pizzas we made tasted better than any we could find in town or elsewhere.

When we didn't work late at the university, Trey would get creative with the ingredients we had in the pantry and pull together something new. Stews and soups were his specialty. He'd start with a bone-in bird, then add sausage, broth, and root veggies, then herbs and a touch of something sweet. The result was always different, and always delicious, savory and herbal and bubbling hot. I'd fill my bowl twice. We'd sit on flimsy camping chairs stoking the wood stove until it was so hot in the little house we'd have to peel off our sweaters and scarves in layers, leaving us sweating in ratty t-shirts. Even with the exhaust spilling smoke through the roof, the whole house always ended up smelling warm and wooded, like a campfire.

Friends from Santiago and Viña and Valpo started to come out to the house to escape the hustle of the city. Practically everyone we knew was interested in seeing the off-grid spot they'd heard about for so long. They visited for *las Fiestas Patrias*, a three-day-long party celebrating Chile's independence from Spain that culminates on the 18th of September, otherwise known as the *Diechioco*. We threw parties for birthdays and parties for holidays. We had dinners and barbecues and student field trips. They'd roll up to the property and pile out of sedans with open *Escudos* in one hand and lit cigarettes in the other. "*Chiquillos!*" they'd shout, throwing their backpacks and tents to the ground and making themselves at home.

After everyone had unpacked their bags, we would load our cars with bags of greasy chips and tall beers in plastic bottles and spend the day at Las Docas. The beaches in Laguna were usually near-empty, and with no rules prohibiting drinking in public, we were free to do as we pleased. The boys kicked around a *futbol* while we played drinking games in Spanish. After a few hours, we'd return home sandy and loud. Someone threw sausages on the grill out back and tended the fire. Someone else counted the beers we had left while someone else remembered they had brought another pack of cigarettes to share. We watched the sun go down beyond the pine trees and stayed up as long as the fire held out. Trey and I snuck away to our bed and as I closed my eyes to sleep, I felt satisfied.

Sometimes Laguna Verde felt like a slice of paradise.

DRY

November, 2012

I stared down at the white buckets full of flower stems and my mind wandered to the last place I had made bouquets. It was on the farm of course, and the flowers were ones I had grown myself that summer. The memory of it felt like a lifetime ago, even though it had only been three years. Today was Lindsey and Boris's wedding.

Lindsey had asked me to help with the wedding bouquets and we started prepping early, sorting through decorations and gathering up peach-colored lilies, daisies and sunflowers in bunches of yellow and red. Trey had stayed home to work but planned to meet me later at the ceremony. The celebration would take place in the *campo*, about twenty minutes outside of Santiago on a *parcela* with a grassy outdoor space and a large enough white tent to fit about a dozen dinner tables plus a dance floor. As we decorated and the hours passed, the ceremony drew closer. I glanced occasionally at my phone to see if Trey had called. He had been given directions to the venue but, without GPS, finding your way to a new place wasn't easy. I started worrying about what would happen if he ended up lost.

The remainder of the bridesmaids arrived and the five of us gathered and changed into our dresses while we excitedly watched through gauzy white curtains as the guests arrived from the city. Lindsey's family had flown in from Washington state and her groom to be, Boris, had his entire extended family in attendance. It was a perfect day for an outdoor wedding, sunny and warm, and everyone was dressed to the nines. As the minutes ticked away and the ceremony was about to begin, I still didn't see Trey. I felt a knot form in my stomach because I knew he was lost and I was going to have to deal with the consequences. After four years together, I still hadn't gotten used to his angry outbursts and how he never cared who was around to witness them. I picked up my phone and, as expected, there were ten missed calls from him. I must have forgotten to turn my ringer on.

I ran to the bathroom so as not to disrupt the happy mood. It felt like the air had been sucked out of the room.

"Hey," I said, "I'm sorry I missed you. We've been busy getting everything ready."

"Yeah what the hell. I've been going around in circles here, I'm totally fucking lost. I'm about to turn around and go home."

"What—no, Trey, don't do that. Hang on, let me get someone to help you." I frantically ran out of the reception building to find Boris's best friend Claudio who was thankfully standing nearby.

"*Por favor* Claudio, Could you help me? Trey is really lost, but I think he's close."

"*Obvio*, Bree," Claudio replied, taking the phone from my nervous hands. The conversation between the two of them went on for a few minutes, but seemed resolved when Claudio hung up.

"All good?" I asked.

"I think so," Claudio replied with a smile, tapping the ash from his cigarette into the grass.

I quickly ran back inside to my friends, and to Lindsey, who was minutes from walking down the aisle.

"Everything okay?" she asked.

"Yeah I think so, Trey's just lost."

"Oh no Bree, are you okay?"

"Yeah, it's all good Linds—don't you worry about it, I'm sure he's close," I replied, knowing I might be lying. I looked down to my buzzing phone—he was calling again.

"Hey, you still can't find it?" I asked quietly even though I knew the answer.

"No this is bullshit, I'm turning around. I've been driving around in a circle for an hour now, I can't find this fucking place."

"Let me get someone else to help you, please don't turn around." I found Boris, the groom, in the crowd and ran to him, calmly assuring Trey as best I could on the way.

"Is Trey still lost?" Boris asked. "I'll help him."

I ran back inside to Lindsey. I knew that if Trey somehow found the location, he'd arrive angry. Soft instrumental music began to echo across the open space, signaling the start of the ceremony. I tried to keep my cool but inside I was frantic and frustrated. *Why did he have to make things hard? Why couldn't we just enjoy a night out?* I should be allowed this, I thought, even though his reminder that "should is a fallacy" rang in my ears.

After we had shuffled our way down the aisle, we waited for the bride to make her entrance and I remembered my own wedding day, and how I was so sure I had made the right choice. Lindsey looked similarly sure now, walking toward us while the crowd quieted to watch her. I smiled back at the photographers and out of the corner of my eye I saw my husband, with his jagged cheekbones, lips tensed in a straight line, arms crossed in front of him. He had a flute of champagne and a lit cigarette in his hand, dressed in the black suit he wore on the day of our wedding.

After the ceremony ended I approached Trey, not knowing if he would be sociable, drinking Trey, or pissed-off Trey, so I tread lightly. There were eggshells to avoid.

"Hey, I'm glad you made it. You look great," I said.

"Yeah, fucking unbelievable." He took a long drag of a cigarette. He must have stopped to buy some, since I hadn't seen him smoke in ages. A smile spread across his face. "Happy to be out of the car." He finished the glass of champagne in one quick sip.

During dinner he continued to drink, which didn't raise any red flags, since we all were, but unlike Trey, the rest of us were taking a bus home. He didn't want to stay the night in Santiago since there was too much work to do at home and the dog needed to be let out, he said. I said goodbye to him after dinner when he returned to the coast.

Trey's idea of fun was very specific, and silly dance parties were simply not something he enjoyed, so after he left I felt free to do what I pleased, dancing and laughing with my girlfriends until 3 AM. That night, I didn't have to be a homesteader, I didn't have to prove anything, and I didn't have to get anything done. I thought: *If I'm the party girl he said I was, I'm gonna lean into it.* We took heavy advantage of the open bar and I got drunk.

The next day I woke up on my friend's couch to a call from Trey. I felt groggy and embarrassed of my hangover and hoped he couldn't tell through the phone. I immediately remembered why I didn't drink like that anymore.

"Bree," he started. "Last night I did something stupid."

I could barely hear him over my pounding heart. "What happened, Trey?"

"I went out last night, I was pissed about the drive, I don't know—just pissed about everything, I guess," he said. "I decided to go to a bar in Valpo. I got drunk and ran out of money so I decided to get money out. But I left our card in the ATM."

"Okay."

"I was angry that I forgot it and didn't have more money and drove home. I don't remember the drive. I don't remember any of it. Those roads, driving drunk—I know. You don't have to tell me how stupid it was, I know that. It was so stupid, so dangerous. I scared myself this morning when I realized what I had done."

"Trey it's okay, it's alright. I'm just glad you're okay."

"There was wine here too, I must have gotten more. I don't remember... I need to stop drinking. I'm done."

"I'll be home soon," I promised, and gathered my things to return to Laguna.

YOU WORRY TOO MUCH

November, 2012

When we met, Trey and I were both drinkers. Not the generally-accepted few glasses a week kind of drinker, either. Our over-indulgence was one of the things we bonded over in the beginning of our relationship and while we had cut back significantly since our days on the farm, a bottle or two of red wine was still the first thing we bought whenever we had any disposable income. We could each put down at least a whole bottle, if not more, or the majority of a 750ml of vodka with grapefruit juice on a sunny afternoon. Inevitably I'd feel guilty and anxious the morning after we drank too much, but it never crossed my mind that it could be a problematic behavior. Alcohol made things fun and light, I thought. It loosened us up. A boring night in the tiny house could turn into a party if we had wine.

And everyone around us had similar drinking habits. Chileans were, in my observation, pretty heavy drinkers. Or at least the Chileans I was acquainted with were. When I spent time with my students outside of class, we went to a bar. Or we'd plan an *asado*, a barbecue, where we'd always make sure there was plenty of beer and red wine to go around. There were alcoholic beverages for every occasion. There was *chicha,* a sweet wine, consumed primarily during *las Fiestas Patrias. Terremotos* (literally, earthquakes) were a deadly mix of grenadine and white wine (called *pipeño*) topped with a dollop of pineapple ice cream. And who could forget the *pisco* sour, a drink so delicious and famous that both Peru and Chile claim it as their own. If we were being social, alcohol was present. During gatherings at our house in Laguna, alcohol brought the disparate groups of Chileans and expats together. We bonded over 40s of *Escudo,* the Chilean national beer, and there was always enough Carménère to go around. If there wasn't, there was someone up for making a quick run to the shop in town to buy more. I looked forward to drinking, the slow buzz of red wine trickling into my brain, turning off my anxiety and worry, the present moment becoming so all-encompassing and interesting that anything outside of it seemed unimportant.

But after his latest incident, Trey was serious about not drinking and it stuck. I quit drinking too, at least when I was around him, which was most of the time. His sobriety further distanced us from other people, since he now wanted even less to do with socializing, and I did my best to accommodate. I was hopeful that things would get better between us. For a while, they did. The sober lifestyle suited us. I saw flashes of the kind of person I wanted him to be—more affectionate, calmer—and clung tightly to them. I'm sure he did the same for me.

After I'd been teaching class at a university one day, a student of mine, Jose, asked if he could give me a Reiki reading. He said that he was a Reiki Master, which sounded significant, though I had absolutely no idea what Reiki was. Jose and I had known each other for a couple years and I trusted him. Like many of my long-term students, he had seen me at my most frazzled: the days when I had to walk the mile to the bus in the pouring rain, the classes after our car had broken down for the tenth time, when I couldn't imagine staying in Chile another minute. I always did my best to maintain my composure, but my students were intrigued by our project so I shared about it often. In truth, our conversations soothed my loneliness.

"Sit down here, in this chair, facing me," Jose said. His voice was quiet and gentle. His English was getting better. "Now, close your eyes. I won't touch you," he promised.

"Okay." I tried to relax my body into the metal-backed chair.

"Reiki is for healing, we use energy. All you have to do is relax," he assured me simply.

With my eyes closed I could sense he had started moving his hands around the space above my seated body. The practice didn't take long, maybe five minutes. Afterward I opened my eyes to see his face looking more serious than I had ever seen it.

"You need to enjoy your life, you worry too much," he said.

"You got all that from the Reiki?" I asked.

"Yes, you try to control things, you have so much stress. You have to work on this," he replied.

I nodded quietly and continued to sit, contemplating the truth of what he had said.

"Just stay here for a while, don't rush to get up and leave," he urged. "Relax here for a minute."

I sat for a moment before realizing I was already late to catch the bus to Viña for my next class. Jose's words echoed in my head. He was right, but I wasn't sure what I was supposed to do about it.

SLOW DOWN
December, 2012

A week before Christmas that year, for the first time in our relationship, we decided that we could afford to exchange gifts. We made a pilgrimage to the local mall in downtown Viña and split up to do our secret shopping. The hordes of people shuffling around the crowded mall bolstered my Christmas spirit and it was calming to be around so many other people all doing the same thing we were. The mall was a haven for me and whenever we could afford it, we'd visit just to walk around, or splurge on the self-serve frozen yogurt with toppings like frozen blueberries and white chocolate sauce. I'd peruse the Zara on the second floor, or spend an hour sifting through the clearance rack at the Paris or Falabella, the two department stores that were the Chilean equivalent to JCPenny and Macy's. In the past I never ended up buying anything, since I knew spending money on unnecessary things like clothing would only make me feel guilty afterward.

But it was Christmas, which was obviously a special enough occasion to buy the types of things we never permitted ourselves, so I snapped up his favorite jeans in gray and a few new t-shirts. He didn't exactly ask for them, but the majority of his clothing was either ripped, stained, or both, and everything had the scent of dirt that no amount of washing could undue. I tucked his presents away in an oversize plastic shopping bag and threw it over my shoulder, practically skipping my way to the Starbucks where we said we'd meet afterward. American Christmas music was playing a little too loud over the speaker of the coffeehouse as I walked in and took my place in the long line that wrapped around the store. This location next to the mall was constantly busy—something about caffeine and consumerism seemed to go hand-in-hand. In my experience, the Chileans who could afford to spend leisure hours at the mall were also drawn like magnets to American-born status symbols like a throwaway cup of five-dollar coffee. I was soaking up the comfort of "home" by way of a Bing Crosby song and a chai latte, waiting for my hopefully happy husband bearing gifts. Despite the subtropical palm trees lining the street and the warm ocean breeze, it actually felt like the holidays.

On Christmas morning we woke up early, poured two large mugs of *mate*, since we were on a health kick, threw our wet suits in the SUV and headed out to La Boca in Con Con, a little beach about an hour north up the coastline that was perfect for beginner surfers. We had decided to start making our own healthy holiday traditions and surfing, something neither of us had much experience with, seemed like a good way to start fresh. We rented boards from a surf shack on the beach and with long boards in hand, headed out to play in the Pacific waves for a couple of hours. I plunged myself in the cold water quickly, ducking under the first wave while clumsily holding onto my board with two hands. The icy water rushed over my head, demanding my attention. I pressed myself onto the board and started to paddle out into the dark blue; Trey was already out and turned around, waiting for a wave. I spun my board around to face the shore and floated, belly down, as wave after wave passed me by. The surf was calm. I cocked my head to the side and watched more experienced surfers catch waves, but didn't feel much urgency to follow their lead. I draped my fingers over the edge to feel the resistance of the water, a familiar comfort. I didn't know if it was the sun heating my dark wet suit or the cold, peaceful water, but my anxiety felt further away than normal, as if I was looking at it from a distance. I could feel my breath slowing as I watched the sun create sparkles in the water around my board. I cast my eyes on Trey, who also seemed to be having a moment of zen even though he hadn't caught a single wave, when a rush of gratitude came over me. How lucky I was to be there, in that place, feeling that way, with him. At that moment I recognized all the years of work it had taken to arrive there. And for a minute, the gift of the present was not lost on me.

At the end of the day we had both only caught one wave each, but we didn't care. We peeled off our wet suits and I tracked sand into the passenger seat of our car with my bare feet. On our way back home, up and down the curvy coastline, we silently sipped our now-cold *mate* from our shared travel mug, holding hands across the stick shift.

Trey finished our outdoor patio in time for summer and in the spirit of trying to prioritize my health, I started doing yoga there every morning while looking out at the ocean. By then I had memorized the sequences our yoga teacher Maria had taught us. I'd practice in the early morning sunshine while Trey explored the land surrounding our house on the mountain bike he had purchased in town from a friend of a friend. He bought me one too, even though I wasn't confident riding on rough terrain. One day he returned, huffing with excitement, after a long ride inland.

"Bree!" he exclaimed, nimbly dismounting his yellow bike. "I found the coolest place. Adrien told me about it and I went to check it out. It's an old factory, you've gotta come with me to see it."

"Where is it? What kind of factory?" I asked.

"It's inland, about a mile or so from a clearing close to Maria and Victor's place. No clue what it used to be but it's full of these perfect old German porcelain tiles. They'd look great in the kitchen," he added. "Let's go tomorrow, we can snag them together."

"Alright, honey," I replied, willing but not exactly anxious to steal old tiles from an abandoned factory.

The next day we threw on our backpacks and rode quickly down the bumpy dirt road toward town, waving to the corner shop owner as we passed him on the street. He must think we're crazy, I thought. Crazy Americans living in Laguna Verde. It was so remote that even Chileans couldn't believe we lived there full time. We rode fast down the steep hill then veered to the right along the road inland towards Curaumilla. We passed the field where our shared garden lived, now brimming with plump heirloom tomatoes, French beans from Adrien's seeds, and multi-colored lettuce. We rode up and up toward a hill where the eucalyptus and pines grew thick, and then into the forest itself. The trail was well worn from past use but overgrown. Looking to the right, through the tree cover, I saw the entire expanse of the rolling hills and valley of Curaumilla below us. The midday light peeked through the branches. The further we went, the more I tensed up: *What if someone found us here?* I'm sure it was someone else's property. There was no one around, as usual, but I worried anyway. Trey rode quickly in front of me and turned around to ascertain my whereabouts every few minutes.

"Are we almost there?" I shouted through the quiet.

"Yup, not much further now."

He slowed and started walking his bike, which was my cue to do the same. A fallen tree blocked the path and tree cover obscured the trail completely.

"Are you sure this is the way?"

"Yup, just did this the other day," he replied, with less patience than before.

The rest of the trail was too difficult to navigate on two wheels so we walked the bikes the rest of the way. I stopped to snap a picture of a fork in the road and Trey said we'd go left.

We came upon the dilapidated concrete building, which looked strange surrounded by the vegetation that had overtaken it. Only the walls of the building remained, there were holes where windows must have been and a roof no longer protected the large metal turbine from the elements. Bright yellow flowers and grass grew in little clumps on the ground between the black and white porcelain tiles of what had been the floor. Trey started identifying the best, most intact tiles, prying them up one by one with a hammer and chisel he had brought in his backpack. All of the tiles showed signs of wear which made them even more beautiful to me. They had a story. I wondered about all the people before us who had worked with them under their feet. After almost two hours of picking and prying, we carefully rode home with two full backpacks of tiles. Trey arranged them in alternating colors, black and white, as a back splash in our tiny kitchen. I wondered if anyone would miss them, maybe people like us, who trespassed to steal beauty from a place we didn't own.

That summer there was more space and time for things that weren't directly related to the house. Not only did we have more free time, we also had more money. We still saved our pesos, and we usually didn't splurge on anything that wasn't related to the project, but if I wanted a tub of fancy face lotion, or a sweater I'd been eyeing for weeks, I bought it. Trey wasn't big on buying his way to happiness. He said he liked creature comforts but didn't need them. Occasionally we'd enjoy a lunch out, or dinner, seafood empanadas from the stand in town. Despite the slight loosening of our purse strings, I worried about money constantly. I was terrified of having to return to the way things were.

We cooked meals together and I learned new things in the kitchen. I plucked the vibrant green kale leaves we had grown in the greenhouse to make smoothies every morning. We created plant beds under the fertile but poisonous *litre* bushes that lined the perimeter of our property. He turned the old greenhouse into a chicken coop and built a larger greenhouse near the edge of the fence where we planted tomatoes, spinach, and arugula for salads. We seeded purple carrots in the newly worked soil and bought a second water tank just for watering everything. We both worked on landscaping on the weekends and in our free moments between classes. On one hand we were taming the land and on the other, we were adding to the wilderness. Life was abundant.

When my friends and family asked how we were, I told them that things were improving. Momentum was the thing that was important and our obvious progress gave us satisfaction. In our relationship, we had become practical partners. Occasionally I'd remember the heat of our courtship and feel nostalgic and resentful that things had changed so much. But usually, we dealt with each other as two people who were accustomed to the bare minimum of physical displays of love.

We watched movies, though the sex scenes made me cringe because we weren't having any. I had been trained to look at affection as frivolous. When I asked for it, he reminded me that his needs also went unmet—his need for more help with the house construction—and so we would both go without. I had hardened myself against the expectation of a soft love, but after years in a sexless relationship, I still craved it. It was a buzzing I couldn't turn off but eventually got used to, like the sound of the refrigerator. Otherwise, our lives looked full. They even felt like it.

Regardless of the state of our relationship, I felt strength in the fact that we both continued to not leave. Our marriage had become a pact to endure all of the shit we had gotten ourselves into. It was love forged out of withstanding. It was a shared story no one could ever know like we did, so we kept choosing not to leave. We focused on the next step. We were taught that good things came to those who busted their asses and we believed it.

ONE OF MY OWN

February, 2013

Violeta had a baby that spring and I walked the short path to their house to meet him the day after he was born. Their place seemed different, the air heavy with the remnants of an important event, the stuff of life. I had never known anyone to have their baby at home and the idea of it was intriguing. It also scared the crap out of me. Violeta looked different too, like overnight she had become a changed woman, a mother. It was a group I obviously didn't belong to. She looked exhausted but unafraid and cradled him in her arms while trying to figure out breastfeeding. It was the first time I had seen someone breastfeed, which sounds crazy but is true, and I tried not to stare. I had never been interested in babies, or kids for that matter. But the way she looked at him gave me pause.

I asked her about birth: Did it hurt? How long did it take? and What's a *doula*, anyway? She introduced me to a new chapter of life. She made birthing and becoming a mother seem like the most natural thing in the world and from then on I became voracious for baby-centric information. *I wouldn't have a clue what to do with a baby*, I thought to myself, but for the first time ever, I imagined myself having one of my own. As time passed, I started feeling a need I was scared to articulate. Maybe it was my deep homesickness or a biological imperative, as Trey would later call it, but the thought of having a child had wiggled its way into my head.

Trey had always told me he never wanted children and I had mostly agreed. Plus, for us to live the kind of life we'd imagined, homesteading off-grid, unencumbered by normal jobs and schedules and "stuff," I had assumed kids were off the table. In my earlier years I didn't fawn over babies or dream of becoming a mother. But as my social circle grew to include women who had children, I noticed their lives having a profound effect on the way I viewed motherhood. Rather than a limitation on freedom, I witnessed real life examples of how mothering could open doors instead of close them. Surprisingly, feeling the shift in my heart around parenting was calming. I gravitated toward the idea of mothering in a way that could be described as earthy, which made sense at the time, since the rest of our lives were the epitome of the term. My new friends birthed their babies at home, breastfed for extended periods of time, used cloth diapers, and wore their babies on their chests. Raising babies that way aligned with how we were living and I envisioned myself doing the same some day. I thought having a child would be cozy and sweet, would provide a love that would fill me up. Maybe, I thought, it would also bring me the attention I so craved.

After months of quietly contemplating, I realized I was serious about wanting a child. I had been dropping hints about my interest around kids but hadn't said anything outright. It was time to have a real conversation, but I was nervous to hear Trey's reaction.

I approached him outside on a Saturday, when he was cutting logs for the fire.

I sat down on a twisted log beside him and got right to the point: "What if I changed my mind about having a baby?" I asked.

"You know I don't want kids, that's not going to change." He continued to chop, raising the ax high into the air and bringing it down with so much force that splinters flew up around him.

"But I really think I want this. I know I always said I didn't want them, but I was so young. You always knew there was a chance I would eventually."

"And I always told you that I would never change my mind. The last thing I want to be is a father."

"But you'd be such a good dad. And having a baby here would be different. I know you don't want to do the suburban dad life, and I get that. You wouldn't have to."

"I know, Bree, but this is not what I want to talk about right now. I'm not going to change my mind about this."

"Fine, Trey. But what do I do?"

"You'll have to go find what you want somewhere else, and I won't stop you."

"Oh that's just great—so you'd rather me leave than have a baby with me?"

"I'm just saying that if I can't give you what you want, I encourage you to get it elsewhere."

I turned my back to him and stomped off into our tiny house. Japhy wagged his tail and slumped down next to me while I sat alone, thinking about what the hell I was going to do. As I sat, scratching the dog's head, I remembered a moment early on in our marriage, a night when we had had too much to drink and ended up arguing about something I couldn't even remember anymore. Trey had ended our fight by throwing a tray of tomato seedlings on the bedroom floor in anger. I remember looking at the ground covered in dirt and seeds and for the first time thinking: *this marriage may not last.* In certain moments, I would return to that feeling, but I never said it out loud.

I didn't say another word about a baby that night, but I found a way to include the subject into conversations every chance I could. Oftentimes our dialogue would disintegrate into a heated argument centered around our unmet needs and unhappiness. Sometimes I could feel Trey softening to the idea but other times he'd maintain his opinion that he was not meant to be a parent. He'd quote a line from a movie we loved wherein Bill Murray, very matter-of-fact, states: "I hated my father and never wanted to be one."

I'll never know what made him change his mind, but months later he did. Perhaps I had worn him down by arguing, or maybe he figured this was the thing that would finally make me happy. It never occurred to me that having a child in Chile would make an already stressful life even more difficult.

"Just one," he said.

"I promise it will be great," I assured him.

ADDITIONS
July 30th, 2013

It was an unseasonably warm day, even though it was technically the beginning of winter. A psychedelic mural stared back at me through the open car window. It was my twenty-eighth birthday and we were driving the forty minutes to my favorite cafe in Valparaiso. After we arrived, Trey ordered coffee and I walked across the street to the pharmacy to buy a pregnancy test.

"Either way, we'll celebrate," I said.

I returned to the café to find him reading and walked directly into the bathroom, squeezed into the tiny stall, and locked the door behind me. I peed on the stick, placed it awkwardly on the back of the toilet, and washed my hands. I felt like I was watching myself try to be normal—*this is how you wash your hands while you wait for your answer, this is how you dry your hands while you think about what happens if it's positive.*

I stayed in the bathroom until the requisite three minutes had passed, then carefully picked up the stick. The tiny purple plus sign was clear as day.

I could feel the effects of adrenaline quickly pulsing through my system: my heart beating in my chest, my hands shaking. I flung open the door with big tears in my eyes and ran out to find him. He was wearing a bright red shirt with Elmo's face on it.

"It's positive!" I laughed and showed him the proof.

"That's great, but let's not get too excited," he said. "It's early."

The cafe sat in the middle of the Plaza Sotomayor, which was the heart of Valpo tourism. People swarmed outside the cafe in groups waiting to start their journey up the hills.

"Yeah, I know, you're right," I replied and looked out the window at the crowds gathering.

We spent the rest of my birthday at home, and though I wanted to celebrate, and scream my excitement from the rooftops, I knew Trey was right to suggest we keep the news mostly to ourselves. In reality it was less a suggestion and more of a statement. And while I was used to letting him make the rules about our lives, I felt empowered by my pregnancy in a way I hadn't before. If he was the expert on building and farming, then I would own the chapter on motherhood. It was the first time in our relationship when I would take the lead.

THE IN-BETWEEN
November 2013

"Mom, can you hear me?" I repeated, nearly screaming through the iPhone speaker in front of my face.

"I'm here, honey," she replied. "We're here sweetheart, we can hear you."

"Okay, ready?" The doctor asked.

We collectively held our breath while mom grasped the bottle of champagne, fingers placed over the cork in preparation.

My midwife's office didn't have an ultrasound machine so I had to travel to a high-rise commercial office building in Viña for my baby's ultrasounds. I had been to this office twice before, the first time at twelve weeks to confirm that I was actually pregnant, and again at sixteen weeks. We were finding out the sex today, and I was praying for a girl even though the last time I was there they told me with 60% confidence that the baby was a boy.

I hadn't seen the same doctor twice, and today yet another doctor greeted us when we entered the dimly-lit ultrasound room. I had told him that we would be video conferencing our family in the United States and asked that he wait until we were able to get them on the line before announcing if the baby was a boy or a girl. He mentioned that he could speak English for the exam, which was helpful since we were asking him to reveal the gender of our baby with my family and closest friends in a grapevine Skype video call. Faye held up her own phone with Kristen and Kristen's sister Jessie on the line. We would all find out at the same time, across five thousand miles.

"Ready?" The doctor asked again.

I nodded my head in agreement. Trey squeezed my hand as the doctor ran the slippery wand over my belly. We fixed our eyes on the large TV screen in front of us and the outline of a skeletal leg appeared. The doctor continued to shift the wand around to get what I assume was a better view, although I couldn't decipher what we were looking at.

"It's a girl," he confirmed to the camera. I could hear the moms screaming through the iPhone.

A girl! Our daughter! I knew my intuition hadn't failed me.

We said goodbye to our family and promised to call back later to continue the celebration. The doctor found her heartbeat next and it echoed through the room's speakers. The first time I had heard her heartbeat, in that very same room at twelve weeks, I was shocked. She wasn't real until that moment; but after it, I was a mother.

The doctor would catch her on the monitor, shifting and squirming. I had started to feel her movements, like bubbles or a butterfly fluttering inside my body. He measured her limbs and the chambers of her heart, among other things. I was only half paying attention, enough to hear him determine that everything looked normal and that we were then free to go. It was like my incredible happiness rendered me unable to focus, but I didn't care. We were having a daughter and she was perfect. How could something so normal feel like such a miracle?

As we left the medical office, I looked to my right to see the sun starting to set over one of Viña's most popular beaches. I cradled my belly with my arm as we crossed the busy intersection lined with palm trees. I had made a habit of showering this baby with affection in whatever ways I could. I wanted her to feel my love.

My focus had entirely shifted to motherhood in the months following my positive pregnancy test. I had a few examples of mothers around me and I watched them closely. Both Violeta and Heather (an effervescent blonde Buddhist from Colorado) had given birth at home. Listening to them retell their birth stories made home birth seem empowering. I read voraciously about natural birth and watched every birth video I could find on the internet. I pored over research on hormones and intervention and medical birth and was convinced that women's bodies were made to birth babies into the world. Never having been to the hospital for so much as a broken bone, the idea of giving birth in a sterile white-walled room seemed scarier than the idea of giving birth in our off-grid home, so I started preparing myself for home birth. I also hadn't visited a doctor's office since arriving in Chile, so when it was time to choose a care provider for my pregnancy, I chose a midwifery practice with the only home birth midwife in the region.

But my introduction to my midwife was less than comforting. On the day of my first appointment, I entered her creaky office through a dark wooden hallway that smelled of lavender and sat quietly on a futon pressed up against the wall for patients to wait. The receptionist asked my name, fired off a number of questions, then turned back to her computer to continue her work. Sensing her disinterest in chitchat, I slunk back to my place near the window and sat down. I fiddled with my too-small sweater (I hadn't invested in maternity clothes) and shifted my attention to a shelf with handmade lotions and soap, turning the expensive bottles over and smelling their sweet contents to busy my hands. The heavy front door swung open and another pregnant woman entered the space. I followed her with my eyes, hoping to exchange a smile and a conversation. Instead, she sat down on the furthest chair from me and stared straight ahead. At least the midwife, Francisca, would be calling for me soon, and for a moment I wished Trey had come with me.

"Briana," the receptionist called out with the Spanish accent I had grown accustomed to hearing.

"*Si.*"

"*Pase.*"

I walked to a small examination room at the end of the musty hallway. The rooms were arranged in a way that felt comfortable and lived-in; this must have been someone's house before it was an office. "I'm Francisca," the midwife said from across the warmly lit room as I entered. She stood about a half a foot shorter than me and wore a look on her face that was inquisitive, though not exactly friendly. I noticed a silver necklace dangling from her neck that depicted a fetus in utero.

I sat down on the edge of the examination chair and she began asking me the basic questions I had expected. She calculated my due date to be early April, then measured my belly and asked me to step on the scale. The only time I weighed myself was infrequently in the gym at the university where we worked. I didn't own a scale for good reason. Thinking about my weight had the ability to send me spiraling into disordered eating territory and I knew myself well enough to avoid it. But there was no avoiding the weight monitoring now, so I stepped on the scale, shifting my weight in an attempt to lessen the blow. Thank God the results were in kilos instead of pounds, since I wasn't about to do the math in my head to figure it out. Uncomfortable, I started nervously rattling off the reasons why I was choosing a home birth in an attempt to fill the space with noise unrelated to my weight. I named all the people I knew who had birthed at home in the hope of giving myself credibility, as if I needed justification to ask for the thing I wanted.

She looked unamused as she took her notes.

Since my one-sided conversation was going nowhere, I stepped off the scale and sat down again, then stared at the posters depicting breastfeeding that hung on the wall. I felt terribly alone in the silence of that room. All I wanted was someone to reassure me, in my native tongue, that everything was going to be alright.

When she finally spoke, she told me that my appointments would be infrequent, since I was low-risk and the pregnancy seemed to be progressing normally. I got up to leave and made my way toward the exit.

"Try not to gain too much weight," she warned, as she watched me go.

BRING IT IN
December 2013

Fourth gear, then into fifth. I passed the seafood restaurant in Con Con. Maybe I'd stop there tomorrow for my usual: fresh melon juice and fried shrimp empanadas. I was so thankful that my first nauseating trimester of pregnancy was over and I had regained my appetite for normal food. I drove north, over the bridge that crossed the Aconcagua River, past Mantagua where the ocean crashed back into view. I watched the water through my driver's side window, sure at least a car or two would pass me going at my unhurried pace. They always passed me. I used to think my slow driving was some kind of failure, but now I didn't care what anyone thought as they whizzed by.

Eventually the road shifted east, snaking north through farmland where cows grazed in fields to my left. Then the gentle beginning of the cordillera; eucalyptus framing the road and wild horses. I arrived at my friend Heather's house that always smelled of patchouli and something cooking. I liked to visit her on the days when my class schedule was light, which was becoming more frequent. She was often singing in the kitchen, cooking Chilean sea bass and quinoa from the farmers' market. We walked to the cove in Ritoque's Playa Chica and made our way across the smooth rocks and boulders that lined the shore. I felt my daughter kick for the first time while I sat on a rock with her watching the waves lapping at the sand.

Every morning I stood in front of the full-length mirror that hung crooked in our bedroom, surprised at how quickly my body was changing. My anxiety, that constant companion that had shown up at the beginning of our house project, had disappeared. It was the best I'd ever felt: strong and purposeful and not alone.

Pregnancy comes with the need to create boundaries, and for the first time in my life I realized I needed to set some. I couldn't give energy to my daughter if I had nothing left to give. The motto that Trey had been drilling into my head for years: *bring it in*, finally felt right.

Bring it in meant stop trying to please everyone.

Bring it in meant focus your energy.

Bring it in meant it's just us out here.

I knew he was right. *Bring it in* was a quiet rebellion. It was the audacity to leave my to-do lists unchecked. I focused on my life and my baby. I thought about the future. I stopped rushing everywhere. I sat on a piece of driftwood Trey and I had lifted from Las Docas and looked out over the gardens we had planted, the hydrangeas in bloom. I slowed the pace of my breathing and felt the breeze come in from the ocean. I hoped my little girl could feel the peace I was trying to cultivate.

We knew we needed more room now that we were adding another person to our family, so Trey started planning an addition on the house. There was plenty of space to build onto our existing sixteen by twenty-four foot house, so Trey framed an additional twelve by twenty-four feet for the new bedroom and another small room. This addition would feel palatial compared to the tight quarters we had grown used to. We bought a power inverter and a second solar panel to supplement our existing solar system, which meant we'd have much more energy flowing through the house any time we needed it. I bought a vacuum. He got a drill. We plugged in the dorm-room-sized refrigerator that we had bought months prior and stored our old yellow cooler and ice packs away, hoping we would no longer need them. At home, Trey and I were unified, moving in the same direction, albeit with different focus points. Mine was the baby, his was the addition, and one served the other. They both had deadlines that were inching quickly closer. I wore my priority in my body while, as per usual, he wore his on his calloused hands.

Trey continued to work quickly. If I left him alone to work for the day, I'd return to a house completely changed. Where our house once consisted of only a kitchen, bathroom and a tiny bedroom, we'd now enjoy a living area with a wood stove and a bedroom that fit a Queen-sized bed. There would be room to spread out. He put down plank flooring and framed out the walls, then finished the red metal roof and added skylights to allow the morning light into both rooms. He painted, constructed shelving units, and built a new box spring and headboard for our bed. Construction was much quicker now that he finally had access to a decent electric drill and saw. He worked from sunup to sundown, like he always did. He was determined to finish before April.

That year, the anniversary of our arrival in Chile coincided exactly with Thanksgiving Day. I couldn't believe that four years had passed since we landed in Santiago with our pockets full of cash and without a clue. The date was a benchmark to gauge our progress and we made it a point to acknowledge the advances we had made. What our anniversaries lacked in celebration they always made up for in gratitude.

"Remember the year we were still sleeping in the tent for Thanksgiving?"

"Or when we had just been robbed?"

"I can't believe we did all of this. Always remember we did all this."

The dark days were behind us. As difficult as it could still feel, it would never be as hard as it was before.

We invited friends over to share in our celebration. It was the first time we had cooked Thanksgiving dinner ourselves, and to make up for years of not celebrating the holiday, we spared no expense on the meal. We bought the largest turkey we could find and stuffed all five kilos of it carefully into the wood stove. Trey performed his chef duties shirtless and we spent the day inside our hot, tiny kitchen stoking the fire and churning out comfort food among our friend group of Chileans and expats that included Pedro and his wife and young children, plus Violeta, Adrien, and their son Lucas, plus Heather and her partner and daughter Flor. They were all new to one another but conversation was easy. In fact, everything felt easy. I was thankful in a way that felt new to me, like I had worked hard for this moment and wanted to savor it, and for a minute there was no need to look forward or back. The present was as good as it had ever been in Chile, or anywhere else for that matter.

Summer eventually swung around again and work stopped for the season. The pace of life slowed in kind and I grew accustomed to the quiet. Every morning I stomped out early into the gardens to harvest greens and prune tomatoes before the brutal sunlight heated up the plants. My pregnant body was out of practice and out of shape for the squatting, kneeling and strange maneuvers farming required and my big belly made for awkward movements and funny balancing between rows.

After the day had become too hot for me to be useful, I'd sit on the porch and listen to the seagulls squawk overhead as they coasted on the ocean breeze. I could smell the sweet German chamomile from the garden when the wind blew. *Colibri*, the biggest and only type of hummingbird I had ever seen in real life, slurped nectar from the bright red and orange flowers of the *tobacco del diablo* plants that were growing wild around the perimeter of the property. *Maqui* bloomed its jammy purple berries next to the blueberry bushes, pomegranate, and artichokes. The water-filled *docas* wove together a carpet of green where there once was only dust. They were just a few of the many native plant species that now flourished on our land due to our diligent propagation, and I felt like a part of the blooming nature that surrounded me.

Every night was quiet; it was just the two of us and the aging dog. To fill the evenings we watched movies that I would download off the high-speed internet at my favorite cafe in Valparaiso. The bar for entertainment had been set low so I scoured the corners of the internet for ones we hadn't seen. I saved dozens of them—old, new, Spanish, English. In our constant search for a new title, I remembered my favorite Spanish-language movie from college, *Sexo y Lucía*. We didn't make it through the opening scene before we both looked at each other with the same realization: we loved the name Lucía. It was the name of our first home in Chile, our little apartment right off of Cerro Santa Lucía. The name was derived from the word *luz*, which means "light" in Spanish. We'd eventually add a middle name, Amada, meaning love. Lucía Amada, love and light. A Spanish name as beautiful as the little girl who would own it.

Thanks to Chile's liberal maternity leave policy, six weeks prior to my due date I went on leave. To keep myself busy during the days without work, I walked every day up and down the red dirt road behind our house. City folks from Santiago had gotten wind of cheap land in Laguna and had started buying up the empty lots in and around our little village. New-builds now dotted the once-barren landscape, A-frames cropped up out of nowhere overnight. I noted their progress with each step on my short daily journey. There was always music in my ears to keep me company, happy melodies that put me in the mood to visualize my birth. I dance-walked down the trail that separated our *parcela* from the newcomers while my birth playlist pumped in my headphones and I held tightly onto my big belly thinking the baby could feel the excitement reverberating through my body. I visualized myself riding the waves of contractions and allowing my body to do what it was meant to, just like I had read about. I wouldn't let my fear get in the way and promised myself I would be brave for her. I prepared like an athlete before a competition, as if I could muscle my way through birth with pure will and stamina. I thought if I could prepare well enough, I could control the outcome. I imagined the woman I would be on the other side of birth, knowing it would change me in ways I didn't yet understand.

Before we knew it, it was fall. And with only a month or less until Lucía was due to arrive, I felt the nervous excitement that accompanies big change. I settled into an even slower pace. I spent my days cleaning and organizing, a woman on a mission, nesting to exert a semblance of control over the uncontrollable.

As my due date approached, Trey asked to accompany me on my daily walks. "Bree, let's get out of the house," he'd say. He seemed tired lately, like the last four years of building had finally taken a toll.

"Alright," I'd say, pulling on my old College of William and Mary sweatshirt that barely fit over my bulging belly.

He crouched down to tie my sneakers even though I hadn't asked him to.

"Thanks honey," I said, and he stretched out his hand to help me up.

"Come on, Japhy." Trey prodded him to join us and we both stumbled slowly out the door.

Stepping outside of the warmth of the house, the air was humid and damp, the clouds hanging so low that it was impossible to see the ocean. Whenever the fog settled into the valley it gave Laguna an otherworldly, mystic quality. Townspeople said Laguna's land was full of rose quartz, which meant its energy was potent and special; the longer I lived there, the more I agreed. And our little piece of land was always so quiet, sometimes eerily so; maybe in the distance you could hear a dog bark or an electric saw, but no other noise pierced the stillness.

Trey led us down the path, past Adrien and Violeta's house, through the locked gate and into the patch of eucalyptus that overlooked the basin of pines below. We peered out over the valley where the invisible ocean flowed in and out. We were each too deep in our own thoughts to break the silence between us but eventually we decided to head back to the house, our lungs full of fresh air and our minds settled.

"The addition looks so great," I said, when the house came into view. "I can't believe it's almost done."

"Glad the drywall is finally up and the new wood stove'll be hooked up soon. Just need to buy a few more parts for the chimney through the roof," he added.

"I can't wait to organize all of her things. I'm picking up the used bassinet tomorrow from a mom in town. Then we should be all set."

I wandered into the greenhouse to check on the plants and crushed up basil leaves between my fingers. I closed my eyes to breathe in the smell and suddenly, I was taken back to the farm and to home and to that summer when we had just met, and it took my breath away. Deep in my belly I felt an absence, like a hollow place inside me where I'd always be missing there. Nostalgia followed me everywhere, even on my best days.

I felt strong but restless, caught in limbo between an old life and a new one I knew nothing about. A suspicion that I was saying goodbye to someone, to the "pre-mother me," had settled in. In my moments alone, visions of the things I might never do again would pop into my mind: staying up all night in a strange city with new people, spontaneously taking a trip, smoking a cigarette in a car with the windows down and the music blasting with my best friend. I thought of all the moments that embodied the fleeting excitement of being young. Though in truth, it had been years since I felt the freedom to act autonomously or to be reckless or do whatever I pleased. The house project had brought with it the weight of a large responsibility and a quick growing-up that I had postponed for as long as possible before it. When I left the States I left that too, and I was realizing that maybe I should have mourned that part of me a long time ago.

I knew, although I couldn't yet understand, that when my daughter was born her happiness would become a requisite for my own; that keeping her safe and healthy would be the driving force of my days, and that Trey's and my own self-interest would widen to include hers.

I also couldn't wait to see her. I couldn't wait to meet the little person who had been living with me, who I felt like I already knew. I had memorized her from the 3D ultrasound photo that I'd pinned to my bedroom wall next to the birth affirmations I had written out in rainbow-colored markers—*she believed she could so she did.*

I wondered if she'd have my big blue eyes or her dad's long skinny legs. Would she eventually share his affinity for dirt and books? Or love the water like me? Would she be serious or silly? It was like waiting to open a Christmas present—I kept trying to shake the box to play out different scenarios about what was inside.

I hired a doula, a Mexican woman named Elena, to provide emotional and hands-on support during my birth and postpartum. Elena was the picture of strong motherhood herself, with long shiny black hair that cascaded down her back and over the colorful flowered blouses she wore. I also enlisted Heather, my loving friend who was studying to become a doula herself, to help during birth.

By the time forty weeks rolled around, I was ready. I knew that if I didn't go into labor by the following week, my plan for a home birth would be impossible since my midwife could only attend births up to forty-one weeks. Lucía's due date came and went. As the days continued on with no sign of labor, the doubts began to creep in. If the midwife couldn't attend the birth, could I do it alone with my doulas? Should I go to the public hospital in Valparaiso instead? I had never been there and the prospect of birthing there seemed terrifying. Birthing alone seemed terrifying. Did I have to make this huge decision? Couldn't someone else make it for me? Through tears I asked Trey what I should do.

"Go outside, look at the moon," he said. He knew that sometimes nature could answer questions we were scared to even ask.

So I wrapped my favorite sweater over my uncomfortable midsection and waddled outside to look at the moon that was now hovering high above my head. "What should I do?" I asked *la luna* out loud. I'll never forget looking up at the moon that night in the sky dotted with stars. I took a deep breath, my nerves calmed momentarily and I trudged back inside.

As soon as my feet hit the wooden planks of the hallway I felt something. I didn't actually believe it, so I walked into the bathroom and sat down, expecting a false alarm. But it was true, my water had broken, or started to. I steadied myself on the white porcelain sink and saw that my hands were shaking.

SURRENDER

April 8, 2014

My gaze rested on a large piece of Styrofoam insulation that was shoved into a space in the unfinished wall of our bedroom. I lugged my heavy body into bed and tried to forget about all the projects that would go unfinished now that the baby was really coming. Trey was starting a fire in the tiny wood stove to busy himself. The butterflies in my stomach would make sleeping impossible, I decided, so I flipped on the television and asked him to join me in bed. I felt like we were the only two people in the whole world, on our little island in the middle of nowhere. We were pretty much always alone and only sometimes lonely, but I didn't feel lonely now.

We switched on the TV and hours passed as I drifted in and out of a dreamless sleep punctuated by waking to scenes of American comedy movies. A scene of Vince Vaughn. A commercial for a probiotic yogurt. Trey stoking the fire again. Eventually, my attention crystallized on a tightening sensation from a part of my body I'd never felt before, somewhere underneath where the baby's head sat. The sun had come up, which I knew because I could see the rays spilling through the plastic cutouts in the ceiling. I was terrified to realize again that it was actually time, even though I had done every bit of preparation I could think of. I wanted to call Elena and Heather but it would be hours before the contractions were intense enough to warrant assistance so I rolled over in bed and sat up, unfortunately too awake now to rest.

Trey made a french press of coffee.

"I think there are ways to speed this up," I said, googling "pressure points to speed up labor," and we both got to work massaging my feet with fervor. He ran his hands on either side of my spine like the website instructed, gently but firmly. I think he was thankful to be put to use.

For lack of anything more constructive to do, we decided to walk the path that ran between our house and Adrien's and the newer lots in construction behind us. I moved slowly, wrapping my sweater over myself whenever I felt the cool air against my skin. Even though we were together, I was starting to feel like I was embarking on a journey where he couldn't join me. We got home and I continued to poke clumsily at acupressure points and contort myself into any position that the internet advised to intensify contractions. I breathed slowly as I forced my hips to make exaggerated circles on the blowup exercise ball, just as I had seen in countless home birth videos.

As the second night of labor descended, the contractions had taken on a different character, more intense and demanding of my attention, so I had Trey call for the doulas. He tended to the fire that had been burning since the night prior and I watched the embers catch and roar in the small wood stove while I shifted and swayed back and forth on the ball to alleviate the discomfort. I could feel each surge coming before it hit—my muscles tensed and I sucked in air, trying my best to breathe normally. Moments later the pain would subside, leaving me panting and shaking. A fog descended and my brain vacated the room, leaving my body to deal with the experience of birth.

The doulas arrived quietly, creeping into the space with gentle words of encouragement. "You're doing it," they said. I felt safer with them there. The contractions were coming more quickly now and I tried to power my way through them, one after another.

By the time the sun came up the next morning, my water had fully broken, which soaked the newly-set wooden floors of the addition. I left the darkness of our bedroom for a change of scenery and walked into the hallway. The sunlight pouring through the windows reminded me that there was life outside of my birth experience, which felt impossible and strange. I remember Elena pouring warm water over my belly in the tiny tub and me crying in her arms from the pain. I remember squatting in the kitchen while Trey held up my aching body. There were stains of blood on the purple yoga mats that had been laid on the bedroom floor.

I remember getting sick, even though I hadn't had anything to eat for over twenty-four hours. The contractions were coming so strong then, one after the other with almost no space to breathe in between. I saw Francisca, my midwife, but who had called her? She checked me and instructed me to lie on my left side to help move the baby into a better position, "sunny side up," Elena translated, which would explain why it was taking so long. I buried my head in Trey's shoulder during each contraction and wailed. Birth felt like a marathon. Heather boiled water because they all said that the baby would be born soon. "Nine centimeters," Francisca said, "almost there."

With my midwives and doulas gathered around me, discussing their next steps, I got into position on my hands and knees, expecting to start pushing. But then, the intensity of my contractions changed. The fog lifted. I regained my sense of time and place. The cliff I was about to jump off of had disintegrated. I had been carried along with the momentum of labor and now I was jolted backwards and I had no idea why.

The women said that sometimes labor stalled but that we would have to get it started again and fast—because my water had already broken, I only had twenty-four more hours until I risked infection. Time continued to pass and blurred again. The pain continued to increase, which was almost unbelievable, since every stage before felt like it had to be the end. My body kept holding on, showing me how much I could take and eventually, a new sensation emerged. I felt an uncontrollable urge to push, every fiber of my being focusing on downward movement. Every muscle of my body was working in unison to accomplish one thing. But something felt off. Francisca checked me again and the baby wasn't descending like she should, despite my cries and screams and pleas to the universe to deliver me, her—us.

Elena brought out a birthing chair, which looked like a wooden stool with a circle cut out for baby-catching. Trey, Heather, and

Elena took turns positioning themselves behind me to support my back and shoulders through the intense contractions while a series of sounds I was unconscious of making escaped my mouth. I voiced growls and screams that came from someplace deep—from animal roots and generations of biology. In between contractions I slept deeply, or so they told me later, only to awake to the next round. For hours we pressed on as the fire roared next to me—the room smelled of blood and in that space it felt like life and death co-mingled. I think everyone who was there started to get nervous.

Francisca checked my heart rate and then my baby's and I looked up to see that the faces of everyone in the room had changed.

"What time is it?" I remember saying. *Que hora es,* someone translated.

"Three o'clock in the morning."

"We have to make a decision," Francisca said. "We'll try one last thing, but if it doesn't work, we have to go to the hospital."

Heather and Elena took a bed sheet and wrapped it around my hips and while I squatted with each contraction, they tried to widen my pelvis by pulling my hips apart. It felt like my entire body was breaking.

And then, after thirty more minutes and for the first time since labor had begun nearly three days before, I said that I was done. I had given every ounce of mental and physical strength I could in the pursuit of birthing my girl at home, but I was completely dilated and she wasn't coming. I knew it was time to go to the hospital. Of all the fears, both spoken and unspoken, that I had during pregnancy, my fear of a hospital transfer was the one I spent the most time worrying about. I knew that if something went wrong during my home birth, I'd have to leave and travel on the bumpy dirt road to be transported to the Valparaiso public hospital forty-five minutes away, a place I'd never been. Not only that, but I knew that my midwife and doulas wouldn't be able to accompany me into the hospital. I was afraid I would have to give birth without my team. I begged them not to leave me there alone.

I hastily pulled on clothing—the first pair of leggings and sweater I could find—then shoved a t-shirt and a newborn onesie into my tote bag. I didn't even pack a single diaper. Walking out onto the lawn felt like being woken up from a trance, or being woken up from a dream, by a bucket of cold water thrown on my face. My only objective was to get to the hospital as quickly and safely as possible. Elena carefully helped me into Francisca's car and Trey followed in ours. I was ten centimeters dilated and the contractions were coming strong as ever and every bump in the dirt road intensified the pain. I held onto the seat to brace myself and tried to steady my body through the twists and turns, all while giving directions in Spanish to Francisca as she navigated us through Laguna. After what seemed like an eternity, we passed through the foggy tunnel and sped into early-morning Valparaiso. I looked around at all of the college students spilling out of the clubs and bars onto Errazuriz Street. It was odd that something so life-changing was happening to me while droves of young people stood five feet away, going about the very normal business of having a good time.

Francisca's little gray sedan stopped abruptly at the ER. We rushed into the reception and Francisca, risking her reputation as a midwife, escorted me inside. I bent over through the contractions, no longer fighting them, and screamed through each one. The hospital nurses quickly led me down a brightly-lit hallway to a room in the labor and delivery ward, but they wouldn't let Trey accompany me, so he sat in the waiting room alone and listened to my cries echoing through the hall.

In the hospital, the responsibility of my birth no longer fell solely on me. I relinquished my authority to the institution and relaxed in knowing that I could finally surrender. I started yelling for an epidural at anyone who came within earshot.

I lay alone in the pink-walled room of the old public hospital, staring at the machine that registered my contractions. I watched the line jump up and down before my body lurched through the height of each one. I had no shame in crying out, I was too tired to be tough. The contractions were so close together that I couldn't speak. A nurse wheeled another laboring woman into the room who looked young and fragile. She didn't pay any attention to me but, more than anything, I wanted to hold her hand in solidarity.

After an indeterminate amount of time, the anesthesiologist finally administered an epidural and immediately the pain went away. I stared at the small circular clock on the wall, 5:30 AM it read, Friday morning. I was so thankful for the relief that I fell asleep. At 7 AM, I woke up and knew it was time. A nurse quietly checked my vitals beside me.

They wheeled me into the birthing room and called in Trey. A pretty young woman with long dark hair introduced herself as the midwife and knelt below me with nurses on each side.

And with the next contraction—Push!—they said in unison, while I squeezed Trey's hand.

I threw my head back and pinched my eyes shut, but the light from the fluorescent bulbs still shone through my eyelids. I held my breath and pushed while everything outside that room faded away.

"She's blonde!" Said the midwife. "One more."

Exhausting every ounce of strength I had left, I screamed and pushed one last time. The midwife cut me to make room for her to leave, cut the umbilical cord that had wrapped itself twice around her neck, then twisted her out from her odd position all in one swift and steady motion. She was finally out! I had never felt such relief. But she didn't cry.

The nurses took over, carrying her little white body away from me and into an adjacent room.

"Is she okay? What's happening?" I screamed in English.

No one said a word. I scanned the faces in the room for an indication of anything.

After an agonizing amount of time, which was probably only about thirty seconds, I heard her sweet cry, so faint, like a purring kitten.

Oh thank God. Thank you, thank you. My baby is alright.

They wrapped her in a hospital blanket and I brought her warm body to my chest as our eyes locked for the first time, then she furrowed her brow as if to say: "Oh, it's you." All my fears were gone in an instant—she was here and she was perfect.

"You were amazing," Trey said, and kissed my forehead.

"Hi Lucía," I cooed.

I gathered her tiny hands in mine and examined her delicate fingers. How could I have made something so wonderful? She seemed too good to be true, her perfect rose-bud lips, her button nose, her wisps of strawberry blonde hair.

"My turn to say hello," her dad said softly.

After the three of us had gotten acquainted, she started to cry so I thought I'd better try to feed her. To my surprise, she latched easily and nursed voraciously as if to say, "That was hard for both of us." I realized we had been working together the entire time.

Soon, the nurses were pushing us out of our love bubble and into the recovery room. Once there, the exhaustion of our long birth hit. Lucía and I slept, finally, my hand holding onto hers across the plastic bassinet.

I woke to find a male nurse standing by my side, asking to change the bedpan underneath me which was a scenario that normally would have caused me to be self-conscious but now didn't matter at all. Birth had temporarily erased every ounce of vanity I had.

Lucía started to stir. "She's beautiful, like a little doll," the nurse said.

He handed her to me and she started to nurse again. I could feel my insides clench and winced, but the memory of the pain of labor was still so present that this pain felt dull in comparison. I stroked the wisps of strawberry blonde hair and kissed her sweet-smelling head. Out of the corner of my eye, I saw Trey moving through the hall so I flagged him down with a tired little wave. He carried a bouquet of flowers underneath his arm.

"These are for you," he said, as he entered the room and planted a kiss on my cheek.

"They're beautiful, thank you."

Another nurse approached us: "You can't come into this room with flowers. When your wife moves to the other room you can, but not here."

Trey turned to face the nurse, anger boiling inside, bubbling up to the surface. Without saying a word, he snatched the flowers from the side table and threw them into the trash, then stomped out of the room leaving me alone. I didn't have the energy to be embarrassed.

I looked at my little girl sleeping. Now, we were in this together. I had done the hardest thing of my life and survived. I felt a deep responsibility for her in my bones, and an unspoken thing that her birth made me face head on. It was shouting inside me and I could no longer pretend not to hear. I could no longer stay in this relationship in Chile. I wasn't sure if I could be brave enough to do the next hardest thing, and either way, I was too exhausted to think about that now.

A few hours later a nurse wheeled Lucía and me into the mother-baby room, which was set up like a summer camp, with ten beds lined up neatly in a row on either side. Each bed was occupied by a mother-baby pair.

I was soon introduced to the unexpected rules of birth recovery in a Chilean public hospital. Mothers were only permitted to drink milk, decaffeinated tea, or still water.

"Water with bubbles hurts your milk," the oldest-looking nurse said, as she did her first rounds. "And no spices, garlic or broccoli. Only bland foods."

I was thankful they fed us, but I had neglected to bring my own utensils, which was apparently the norm. I had to ask the mother in the bed next to me to watch Lucía so I could use the bathroom and after I carefully waddled down the hall, I realized we were also supposed to bring our own toilet paper. I was accustomed to bathrooms in Chile being without, but hadn't thought about packing any in our mad dash to the hospital the night before.

Since Trey was only permitted to be with us during the short visiting hours in the morning and evening, I was mostly on my own to figure out our new baby. The lights were always on, which made sleeping difficult if not impossible. Beeps and crying were the soundtrack of the first days of our new life. And unlike the friendly midwife, the nurses who were caring for us seemed to have been beaten down by the constant chaos. They moved brusquely around us, chastising the new mothers for all the things we were doing wrong. "Don't lay her down like that, she'll choke," one said to me as I placed Lucía down on her back to sleep. "That's how babies die."

It was nothing like the introduction to motherhood I had expected.

Then the fire started.

FIRE IN VALPARAISO

April 12, 2014

The day after Lucía was born, a wildfire erupted in the hills of Valparaiso. The flames grew, uncontrolled and raging through the region where ten women, including me, sat with our new babies. We could smell the smoke as it crept through the cracks in the aging hospital. Valparaiso was declared a disaster zone. We were forced to close all the windows in the ward to prevent the smoke from getting in and as the lights flickered on and off and the generator turned on, we were warned that if the flames grew closer, we might have to evacuate. I sat wide awake at night listening to the babies cry and the helicopters fly overhead, dumping water on the interminable fire. When they sent in the Chilean army to take control of the city, two of the women in our shared room were told their homes had burned along with all of their belongings. Over the course of two days, the fire swept through over 1,700 acres, destroying more than 2,500 homes in its path. The news proclaimed the fire was the most catastrophic in the city's history.

But the fire was finally put out, two days after Lucía was born. After two nights in the hospital we were released to go home. The unmistakable smell of smoke assaulted us as Lucía, Trey, and I left the hospital grounds and made our way to the car outside. Marines sent in by the government policed the smoky streets. I've never carried anything so carefully as I did my brand new baby as I set foot outside the hospital for the first time. While our car slowly snaked through the streets, we stared in sadness at the destruction the fire had created around us. We later found out that more than eleven thousand people had been made homeless by the fire. The embers were still burning in the hills.

The weeks and months that followed were a blur of sleepless nights and breastfeeding. Life with a crying baby in a tiny house. I called my mother every morning while Trey went off to teach because I couldn't stand to be alone with my thoughts. My anxiety, which had been nonexistent in the months prior, came roaring back with a vengeance. I had a fierce and irrational desire to protect Lucía from harm and I saw the potential for harm everywhere. My abundance of love for her overwhelmed me. I imagined horrible things happening to the baby, which felt like a movie playing vivid horror scenes while I was awake. Every misstep could bring disaster. I thought maybe I was an awful mother, or that I was going crazy. I had to train myself to inject humor into each violent scenario I imagined so that my visions didn't throw me into a complete panic, but most of the time they still did. I didn't want to put words to my intrusive imaginings because it would only make them more real, so I kept my problem to myself. I tried desperately to be okay.

My days were consumed with nursing and changing diapers and wearing our baby who would cry every time I put her down. In between the feedings I would start on the pile of cloth diapers, which seemed to grow by the minute, or wash our dishes by hand. Chores felt tiresome and more difficult than before, as if I were wearing weights and trudging through quicksand to complete even the simplest of tasks.

Having a brand new baby magnified the challenges of homesteading on a little piece of far-out foreign land. A trip to the grocery store was an epic journey. Needing to get our drinkable water delivered made me nervous. Would we have enough electricity to run the refrigerator? What would we do when the rains came? I could only see the scarcity of our resources. I threw all my love, time, and energy into the baby. There were no bottles, or formula, so the responsibility of feeding Lucía belonged to me. And at night, she slept on my chest, so nighttime wakings were my job too. Any bit of world that Trey and I had shared before she arrived, any amount of space I held for him, was now hers. My life shrank to the size of one tiny infant. I started to get vocal about the decline of my mental health, though I kept the shameful specifics to myself. Trey was becoming more obviously annoyed by my inability to tame my panic.

Trey kept his head down and himself busy, since caring for Lu was mostly my domain. He would ocassionally help or hold her, but since she would only calm for me, he doubled down on other things. For the first time in our relationship, Trey deffered to me. I'm sure he felt left out. He finished off the bedroom like he said he would and continued to grow the farm business, schlepping his leafy greens into Santiago for as many customers as he could.

But life with Lucía wasn't all hardship. We enjoyed her during little moments at home. Drinking our morning coffee in bed, we'd love on her, Trey squeezing her chubby thighs, stoking the fire while we watched her smile for the first time. I loved taking her out in public together to get away from the confines of our house. It felt normal—me with my diaper bag and him holding Lu on his lap while we shared a plate of fries.

At six weeks old, Lucía choked on breast milk while I fed her and she stopped breathing for a moment. I called Adrien and Violeta, who rushed to our aid, and we decided we should head to the emergency room. Once we arrived, the doctor presented me with two options: leave her with them for a couple of days while they ran tests, or bring her home and risk infection. My exhausted, anxious mind couldn't arrive at a reasonable decision. I obviously couldn't leave her alone in a Chilean hospital, but could I risk bringing home a sick baby? While my frazzled brain weighed my options, Trey made the choice for us: "No way are we leaving her here," he said, stood up, and charged out of the hospital room. I followed behind him, Lucía in tow, wondering if I had overreacted by bringing her to the doctor. I nestled into the back seat of the car next to my now calm infant, questioning my ability to make any decision at all. I felt like I couldn't trust anyone. It felt like the last straw.

Before Lucía was born, no matter what happened, when we were penniless, robbed, homeless, stealing, or grieving, I trusted that Trey knew what to do to get us out of it. For five years, I had done everything I could to put the project first. We had opted out of a regular life in favor of an adventurous one. I thought that if I continued to suffer through it, to build something big and different, I could finally be enough. Maybe then I could guarantee my place in the world, maybe I could earn the respect and love of others, including him. Before her, if my happiness was the collateral damage of a project bigger than me, I was okay with that.

But now, in the presence of my daughter, my heart pointed to my own happiness and said "This matters too." I would need to accept who I was and who I wasn't, and stop believing those things made me needy or overwhelming. My search for comfort wasn't silly, it was natural. My social nature wasn't codependency, (or at least not always,) it was a piece of the fabric of who I was. If I was going to raise Lucía to embrace her whole self I'd have to allow myself to do the same.

I was no longer the twenty-two year old fleeing from home, searching for adventure, begging for someone to tell her which way to go. I had sacrificed the life I knew, lost it, and gained everything. I had become a woman I was proud of. The accomplishment filled me up. I had rebuilt my foundation with grit and stubbornness and birth, but I was exhausted. It was time to work on cultivating a home inside myself in a place where everything wouldn't feel so damn hard.

The following morning I woke up with the sunrise, Lucía sleeping on my chest. I cradled my little girl in the crook of my arm and walked the perimeter of the property—it really had come together. We really had done the thing we set out to do. But I felt no sense of relief because I knew the hard would keep coming if I stayed. Could the good outweigh the bad? My thoughts ping-ponged in my brain as I tested out the scenarios and choices that lay in front of me. Should I stay and try to survive or return to the States to start over? Would he come or would he stay? Would my longing for home sit forever under my eyelids, pressing up against my view of the world, distorting my present with nostalgia and comparison?

I looked down at her, the person who was now the most important thing in the world, and knew I had a choice to make.

I watched the sun turn the big sky pink; streaks of orange hovered above the peaks of the pines; winter would be over soon. I breathed in the clean ocean air. Laguna had become a part of me, of us. The house project had been our entire existence for so long, I wasn't sure how I would live without it. Would anything ever be as beautiful as standing in the middle of a life built from scratch, a life chiseled out of an idea, one clawed and pushed through until it looked right? But as proud as I was, I wasn't sure the idea was ever mine in the first place.

What would become of us? I couldn't imagine a version of the future where Trey would forgive me for leaving. The house project, he would explain later, was not something outside of him. The house was him—blood, sweat, and a million driven nails. I could stay for him or I could leave for me.

"*Eres Chilena, mi amor,*" *You're Chilean, my love,* I told her in a language that was no longer so foreign, and kissed her head.

And so, "I just need a break," I explained to him, in a way that tried to minimize the weight of what was really happening.

"You're not coming back," he replied.

LISTEN
May, 2019

I left Chile on August 14, 2014, with my four-month-old strapped to my chest, dragging an old red suitcase full of cloth diapers and not much else. I wasn't surprised when Trey didn't beg us to stay, and I wasn't sure I even wanted him to. After I had settled in back home with Lucía, we spoke only through messages and emails, back and forth, blaming and apologizing. He didn't want to see us on video calls and I knew he had his reasons. When he was angry it was simpler for me too, because it removed the nuance of the situation: he was wrong and I was right. My friends and family asked, *How can he stay?* But I understood. I was one of only two people who understood why the house project had meant so much.

While I waited for him to come back, or decide not to, I slowly got on with my life. For two years we lived at my mom's condo while I worked and saved money. At first, even the simplest things felt luxurious, like the soft bath towels that smelled of expensive fabric softener. I buried my face in their sweet scent of artificial flowers.

I'd spend my morning commute wrestling with the idea of my marriage, turning over every rock to see if there was something I had missed. I vacillated between feeling committed to him, or the idea of him, and wanting something entirely different. I asked him if he thought we could build a new life together and be happy, and he'd always have a different reply. He was realistic, he said, and he was sorry.

Nearly eight months after I returned, Trey begrudgingly moved back to the States. He wanted to try to be the kind of person I needed him to be. But we soon found that we couldn't change who were were to one another. Like a worn-down trail you've tread a million times, we couldn't start over on a different path, at least not together.

He managed to sell our house to a neighbor who paid us a fair price and we split the proceeds of the sale to invest in our separate futures. It was alarming how easily our old life was stripped away, wiped clean. Sometimes I felt like it only existed in my memory. As time went on, I realized I would be carrying the story of the house project alone, since Trey no longer shared his life with me. Remembering it all was too heavy a burden for only one person, but we did share her.

Co-parenting Lucía was a strange and lonely experience. On the days when she was under my care, I tried to fill every moment with as much love and memory-making as possible. And when she left to spend time with her dad, I didn't know what to do with myself. I'd shuffle from room to room, picking up her toys and hating the silence of my empty house. The years passed quickly but watching her leave never got easier.

§

"Mama!" She screams with excitement, grabbing my hand and dragging me toward her. It's Tuesday—my turn to pick her up from her dad's house. "I want to show you the pigs."

Her strawberry blonde curls catch the sunlight—she always comes back from the farm with clean hair and dirty feet. Trey looks only slightly annoyed that a trek up to the pigs will prolong the usually quick child pickup, so I agree to follow her. I look around; it's not often I'm invited in. I see that everything is how it always was: the seeding greenhouse, the flower house, the blueberries now sprouting their green leaves in anticipation of summer.

I let her lead me, as if I hadn't lived there too, as if I hadn't been the one plodding up the hill to feed the pigs ten years earlier. She reaches out a tiny hand to pat the nose of her favorite one. "They eat all of our leftovers, mama," she explains with a proud five-year-old smile. "I feed them every morning." She is capable beyond her years, passionate about a car sing-along, about digging in the dirt and dancing outside on a rainy summer day. She embodies the best of both of us.

"Mama, can we stay here a little longer?" she asks. The guilt of my choice stings a little.

"No, *mi amor*," I reply, "we have to get home." As I pack up her things and buckle her in, he kisses her goodbye and promises to take care of the pigs in her absence. I adjust my rear view mirror as we leave and catch a glimpse of the zinnias, a flash of color that sparks a memory from before we went south.

Someday I'll tell her everything.

ACKNOWLEDGEMENTS

My deepest gratitude goes out to my loving family and friends. Your support and willingness to accompany me through every iteration of this book have been invaluable. It was your belief in me that gave me the confidence to finish and publish this story.

The journey of writing this book has spanned nearly five years, filled with countless hours stolen between bedtimes, work deadlines, and the very real work of maintaining our home. To Flynn, thank you for the space to finish this project and for your unconditional love, embracing not only who I am now but also who I've been.

And to everyone else who's played a part in this wild ride, whether you're mentioned here or not, thank you from the bottom of my heart.

ABOUT THE AUTHOR

Briana Lawrence resides in the suburbs of Philadelphia, PA with her husband and three children. A passionate writer, Briana is drawn to the power of storytelling to connect with people and provide comfort through shared experiences. She hopes to continue sharing her stories with the world.